# Meet the Cockatiel

■ The cockatiel is a member of the parrot family.

■ The cockatiel originated in Australia and is sometimes called the quarrion, the weero, the cockatoo parrot, or the crested ground parrot.

■ The word cockatiel is derived from either the Dutch *kakatielje,* which means "little cockatoo," or the Portuguese *cocatilho,* which means "small parrot."

■ The cockatiel's small size (12 inches tall and weighing about 3.5 ounces) makes him appealing and approachable for children and adults.

■ One of the most recognizable features of the cockatiel is his crest.

■ Lots of cockatiels have a distinctive color combination of gray, white and yellow.

■ ...atiels have been described as curious, adaptable, clean, and entertaining.

■ The cockatiel can live up to 20 years and is easy to maintain and affordable to keep.

■ Although they are not particularly noted for their talking abilities, most cockatiels can learn to whistle simple tunes. They are not particularly noisy.

■ The cockatiel can be a demanding pet, requiring his owner's regular attention as well as a stimulating environment.

■ Cockatiels need to be fed a variety of seeds and nuts along with fresh fruits and vegetables.

*Consulting Editor*
## PAMELA LEIS HIGDON

*Featuring Photographs by*
## ERIC ILASENKO

**Howell Book House**
Hungry Minds, Inc.
909 Third Avenue
New York, NY 10022
www.hungryminds.com

For general information on Hungry Minds'
products and services please contact our
Customer Care Department within the U.S. at
800-762-2974, outside the U.S. at 317-572-3993
or fax 317-572-4002.

Library of Congress Cataloging-in-Publication
Data
The essential cockatiel / consulting editor,
Pamela Leis Higdon;
featuring photographs by Eric Ilasenko.
          p.   cm.
     Includes bibliographical references (p. 88)
and index.
     ISBN 1-58245-027-7
     1. Cockatiel.   I. Higdon, Pam
     SF473.C6E77   1999              98-45862
     636.6'8656—dc21                 CIP

Manufactured in the United States of America
10  9  8  7  6

*Series Director:* Michele Matrisciani
*Production Team:* Carrie Allen, Heather Pope, and
     Donna Wright
*Book Design:* Paul Costello
*Photography:* Eric Ilasenko

## ARE YOU READY?!

☐ Have you prepared your home
and your family for your new
cockatiel?

☐ Have you gotten the proper
supplies you'll need to care for
your bird?

☐ Have you found a veterinarian
that you (and your cockatiel) are
comfortable with?

☐ Have you thought about how
you want your bird to behave?

☐ Have you arranged your schedule to accommodate your bird's
needs for exercise and attention?

*No matter what stage you're at with
your cockatiel—still thinking about
getting one, or he's already part of the
family—this Essential guide will
provide you with the practical information you need to understand and
care for your avian companion. Of
course you're ready—you have this
book!*

# ESSENTIAL

# Cockatiel

## SIGHT

Cockatiels, like all birds, have a well-developed sense of sight. They can see detail and discern colors. Because their eyes are located on the sides of their heads, cockatiels rely on monocular vision, which means they can use each eye independent of the other.

## SOUND

The cockatiel's ears are large holes located under the feathers behind and below each eye. Cockatiels have about the same ability to distinguish sound waves and determine the location of the sound as people do, but seem to be less sensitive to higher and lower pitches than their owners.

## TASTE

A parrot's mouth works a little differently than a mammal's. Cockatiels have fewer taste buds, which are located on the roof of their mouths, not on the tongue like ours.

## TOUCH

The cockatiel has a well-developed sense of touch. Parrots use their feet and their mouths to touch their surroundings, to play and to determine what is safe to perch on or chew on.

## SMELL

Cockatiels seem to have a poorly developed sense of smell because smells often dissipate quickly in the air (where flying birds spend their time).

# CHAPTER ONE

# The Perfect Cockatiel

Cockatiels make wonderful pets for individuals or families. Their size (12 inches tall and 90 to 110 grams [about 3.5 ounces]) makes them appealing and approachable for children and adults.

Cockatiels offer their owners all the charm and personality of their larger cockatoo cousins without the inherent noise and other problems that can come with the larger birds. Cockatiels can live as long as 20 years; they are easy to maintain and are affordable to keep.

Although they are not known for their talking ability, most cockatiels can learn to whistle simple tunes and may also learn a few words.

## IS A COCKATIEL THE PET FOR YOU?

Before you bring your new cockatiel home, consider these questions: Do you like animals? Do you have time to care for one properly? Can you have pets where you live? If you've answered "yes" to all these, you're a good candidate for bird ownership.

You'll also need to consider the following: Do you mind a little mess

*Cockatiels thrive on companionship, and a happy bird is one who gets attention from his owner.*

2

(seed hulls, feathers and discarded food) in your home? Do you mind a little noise (cockatiels sometimes greet the dawn and bid adieu to the sunset with a typical call) as part of your daily routine? Are you allergic to dust and dander (some people find that cockatiels make them sneeze)? If the answer to these questions is "yes," perhaps you should consider another kind of pet. If the answer is "no," however, a cockatiel may be just the bird for you!

It is recommended that pet owners acquire young, hand-fed cockatiels, if possible. The birds are weaned and eating on their own when they are about 8 weeks old. Most breeders and pet stores have young birds available from April to September.

To maintain their lovable personalities, cockatiels need companionship. If you can't devote about an hour of physical interaction and play every day to your bird, either don't adopt him or make sure he has a cockatiel companion. That half hour could be spent cuddling on the couch while you watch a sitcom, eating breakfast or dinner together or having your bird on a play gym in your bedroom while you get ready in the morning. You can also spend time with your bird while making safe toys for him (such as stringing Cheerios or raw pasta on some bird-safe, vegetable-tanned leather or cotton twine), trick training him or building him a play gym.

## THE BOTTOM LINE

Some things you'll want to think about before you become a cockatiel owner are:

- the cost of the bird
- the cost of his cage and accessories
- the cost of bird food (seeds, formulated diets and fresh foods)
- the cost of toys
- the cost of veterinary care
- the amount of time you can devote to your bird each day
- how busy your life is already
- who will care for the bird if you go on vacation or are called out of town unexpectedly
- how many other pets you already own
- the size of your home

## WHERE TO GET YOUR COCKATIEL

Cockatiels can be purchased through several sources, including classified newspaper advertisements, which are usually placed by private parties who want to place pets in new homes; bird shows and marts, which offer breeders and buyers an opportunity to get together and share their love of birds; and pet stores. Stores that sell livestock are listed as pet stores in the phone book, while those that offer only food, toys, treats, cages and other pet-care accessories would fall into the category of pet supply stores.

### *What's That Band Mean?*

As you select your pet, you may notice leg bands on the cockatiels you're looking at and may wonder why the birds are wearing them. Bird bands serve several purposes. First, they help identify a particular breeder's stock. They can also help establish an age of a bird because many of them have the year of hatch as part of the band's code. Finally, some states require that pet birds be banded with closed, traceable bands

3

so the origin of the bird can be determined in an effort to reduce the number of smuggled birds that are kept as pets in the United States. Smuggled birds can carry disease. Although this requirement doesn't apply to cockatiels, it is an indication of things to come in aviculture.

While most cockatiels can wear leg bands successfully for their entire lives without injuring themselves, you may want to discuss removing your bird's leg band with your avian veterinarian. Occasionally a bird catches a band on its cage, cover or toys. This can injure the bird or cause it to lose a leg. If you opt to have the band removed, keep it in a

safe place in case you ever have to prove that your cockatiel was raised domestically.

## Hand-Fed or Parent-Raised?

Regardless of where you purchase your cockatiel, try to find a hand-fed bird. Hand-fed birds usually cost a bit more than parent-raised ones, because they were raised by people. This process eliminates the bird's natural fear of humans and ensures that he will bond with people. You must be willing to spend time playing with and handling your hand-fed cockatiel every day to keep him tame.

## SELECTING YOUR COCKATIEL

Once you locate a source for hand-fed cockatiels, it's time to select your pet.

First, observe the birds that are available for sale. If possible, sit down and watch them for awhile. Take note of birds that seem bolder than others. Consider those first, because you want a curious, active, robust pet, rather than a shy animal that hides in a corner.

*Cockatiels that were hand-fed from an early age tend to bond better with people.*

*A clean, secure cage; varied diet; and regular attention are just some of the elements that make for success-ful cockatiel ownership.*

5

If possible, let your cockatiel choose you. Many pet stores display their cockatiels in colony situations on play gyms, or a breeder may bring out a clutch of babies for you to look at. If one bird waddles right up to you and wants to play, or if one comes over to check you out and just seems to want to go home with you, he's the bird for you!

# A COCKATIEL OF A DIFFERENT COLOR

Before choosing a cockatiel, a potential owner should be aware of the many varieties available. Thanks to ever-changing breeding techniques, the original gray cockatiel has been mutated, or changed, to reflect differences in color and wing marking. Which one is your favorite?

## Color Mutations

Color Mutations are a popular topic with cockatiel owners. In its simplest terms, a mutation is a change. When speaking of cockatiels, mutations refer to dramatic or subtle changes in color or wing marking these little birds have gone through over the years.

A bird's genetic makeup (or genotype) also determines its

physical appearance (or phenotype). Birds can have similar outward appearances, yet have different genetic backgrounds. Chromosomes are further subdivided into sex chromosomes (cockatiels inherit one pair of these) and autosomes (the chromosomes that determine all the bird's other characteristics).

Dominant traits suppress all other traits. These hidden traits may reappear in subsequent generations. Recessive traits show themselves only when two birds that both carry the recessive trait are bred. Otherwise, recessive traits are hidden by dominant traits.

*In their natural setting, cockatiels are gray birds with yellow crests and faces that are accented by bright orange cheek patches.*

Normal birds are described as homozygous, which means they possess only the genes for the revealed color. Split, or heterozygous, birds carry hidden color traits that may show up in subsequent breedings.

Sex-linked traits are traits that depend on an offspring's gender to appear or disappear. Examples of this type of mutation in cockatiels are the pearl, the cinnamon, the lutino and the albino. The other mutations—pied, silver, white face and fallow—are autosomal recessive, which means that the gene responsible for the mutation is not carried on a sex chromosome.

The last bit of genetic information you need to know before we start our discussion of color mutations is that sex chromosomes in male cockatiels are referred to as ZZ and females are ZY, which differs from the XY used to designate human male chromosomes and XX for human females.

## In the Wild

In their natural setting, cockatiels are gray birds with yellow crests and faces that are accented by bright orange cheek patches. Males are usually dark gray and have solid-color tails and flight feathers. Females have traces of yellow on their faces, and they have yellow bars on their tails and yellow spots on their flight feathers. From these gray birds came the first cockatiel mutation, pied, in 1949, and mutations are still being developed today. The most recent, yellow face, came about in the early 1980s.

## Pied

The pied was developed in California in 1949. These birds show a combination of white, gray and yellow feathers that can range from resembling a normal gray bird to a bird that has almost no gray feathers on her body.

The ideal pied male is clear (meaning it has no melanin) with brown eyes, gray feet, beak and legs, and his plumage shows irregular white patches. Pied females resemble normal gray females, except that their plumage, too, shows white patches. Females can be split to pied, which means they look like normal birds but produce pied chicks.

*The pied cockatiel shows a combination of white, gray and yellow feathers.*

## Lutino

One of the most popular mutations is the lutino. These whitish-yellow birds were first seen in Florida in 1958, and the mutation resulted from a pair of normal-looking birds. The lutinos were first called "Moonbeams" after the breeder, Mrs. Moon, who established and popularized the mutation.

Lutino birds lack melanin in their feathers, eyes, beak, feet and nails, which accounts for their light yellow coloring and red eyes. Lutino males are often whiter than females

## THINGS TO LOOK FOR WHEN CHOOSING A HEALTHY COCKATIEL

- bright eyes

- a clean cere (the area above the bird's beak that covers his nares or nostrils)

- upright posture

- a full-chested appearance

- actively moving around the cage

- clean legs and vent

- smooth feathers

- good appetite

Simple steps, such as providing a varied diet and a stimulating environment, make for a happy cockatiel.

*This four-month-old baby is an example of a male Lutino cocaktiel.*

and lack yellow spots on their flight feathers and yellow bars on their tails. The males have red-orange cheek patches, red eyes, pink feet and legs, gray beak and yellow crest. The females' tail bars and wing spots look yellow against a white background in this mutation.

### *Cinnamon*

Cinnamon was developed in Belgium in the late 1960s. Cinnamon birds resemble normal gray birds, except that the black melanin in a normal gray bird has been replaced with brown melanin in the cinnamon bird. The cinnamon's feathers vary from tannish (if they are male) to brownish (if they are female) rather than gray, and their legs and eyes are lighter in color. Chicks hatch with red eyes that darken within a week. This mutation is sometimes referred to as the Isabelle by European breeders.

Although it was first seen in New Zealand in the 1950s, the recessive silver died out there, only to resurface in Europe in the 1960s. The other silver mutation, the dominant silver, was discovered by accident by a breeder who was looking for new stock in a British pet shop in 1979. This bird was eventually bred back to its mother to further the line. Silvers can be described as paler, browner birds than the normal gray cockatiel. Silvers also have black eyes and legs. Male silvers can range in color from smoky brown to silver with the traditional yellow face, while females are dark brown birds.

## Pearl

Pearls first appeared in Germany in 1967. This mutation is known for the scalloping that can appear on a bird's breast, wings or back, which is caused by gray feathers that have yellow centers. The eyes of the pearl are black, and its beak, feet and legs are gray.

When this mutation was first developed, pearl males lost their pearl markings after their first molts and looked like normal grays at the age of six months, but breeders in the United States have created pearl males that maintain their pearl plumage into adulthood.

## White Face

The white face mutation was first seen in Holland in 1969. As its name implies, white-faced birds

have no yellow or orange on their faces. Instead, they resemble black-and-white photographs of normal cockatiels.

*An example of a cinnamon pearl cockatiel with a white face.*

## Fallows

Fallows were developed in Florida in 1971. These red-eyed soft brown birds have been described as being gray-brown by some breeders, while others liken the color to milk chocolate. The most noticeable color change appears on the primary wing feathers of the fallow.

## Albino

Two existing mutations—the white face and the lutino—were used to develop the albino (which some breeders refer to as the white face/lutino) in Germany in 1980. These pure-white birds have red eyes. They lack not only melanin, but also carotenoid pigments, which is what gives the cockatiel its characteristic cheek patches. Both sexes are completely white with ruby or red eyes.

## Yellow Face

The most recent mutation to develop is the yellow face. In this mutation, which was introduced in the United States in 1992, the orange cheek patches of the normal gray have been replaced with yellow patches.

Cockatiel breeders can combine the mutations described above into a number of different possibilities. It is possible to breed birds that combine two, three or four mutations.

# TEN STEPS TO BETTER BIRD CARE

First, provide a safe cage in a secure location in your home. This cage should have appropriate bar spacing for a cockatiel and accessories that are designed for cockatiels. Locate the cage in a part of your home where you and your family spend time in regularly; this will help your bird feel part of your daily routine.

Next, change the cage paper, food dishes and water bowls daily (be sure to wash the bowls thoroughly with soap and water and rinse them completely), and scrub the cage every week to protect your pet from illness and to make his surroundings more enjoyable for both of you.

Third, clip your bird's wings regularly to ensure his safety. Cockatiels fly well and if yours escapes your home, he will fly too fast to recover him. Be particularly alert to new wing feathers that grow in following a molt. Close windows and doors securely before you let your bird out of his cage. You should also keep your bird indoors when he isn't caged and ensure that your pet doesn't chew on anything harmful or become poisoned by toxic fumes from overheated nonstick cookware, cleaning products and other household products.

Fourth, offer your cockatiel a varied diet that includes seeds and pellets, small portions of fresh vegetables and fruits and healthy people food. Provide the freshest food possible, and remove partially eaten or discarded food from the cage before it has a chance to spoil and make your pet sick. Your bird should also have access to clean, fresh drinking water at all times. You may need to change the water several times a day. If you notice food and bird droppings in the water, move the bowl away from perches.

Next, establish a good working relationship with a qualified avian veterinarian early on in your bird ownership (preferably on your way home from the pet store or breeder). Don't wait for an emergency to locate a veterinarian.

Sixth, take your cockatiel to the veterinarian for regular checkups, as well as when you notice a change in his routine. Illnesses in birds are sometimes difficult to detect before it's too late to save the bird; preventive care can help head off serious problems before they develop.

Seventh, maintain a routine for your cockatiel. Make sure he's fed at about the same time each day, his playtime out of his cage occurs regularly and that his bedtime is well established.

Eighth, provide an interesting environment for your bird. Make him feel that he's part of your family. Entertain and challenge your bird's curiosity with a variety of safe toys. Rotate these toys in and out of your bird's cage regularly, and discard any that become soiled, broken, frayed, worn or otherwise unsafe.

Ninth, leave a radio or television on for your bird when you are away from home. A quiet environment can be stressful for many birds, and stress can cause illness or other problems for your pet.

In his natural habitat, a lack of noise indicates the presences of a predator or other danger. Your pet's instincts remain the same as his wild relatives; silence will stress him.

Finally, pay attention to your cockatiel on a consistent basis. Devote time each day to your pet bird, and soon the two of you will have formed a lifelong bond of trust and mutual enjoyment.

# CHAPTER TWO

# Homecoming

Give your cockatiel a chance to gradually get used to your family's routine after you bring her home. Your new pet will need time to adjust to her new environment, so be patient. After you put your cockatiel in her cage for the first time, spend a few minutes talking quietly to your new pet, and use her name frequently while you're talking.

Avoid looking directly into her eyes. Because you are larger, she may view you as a potential predator. Your direct gaze may frighten her.

## ADJUSTMENT TIME

After a couple of days, your cockatiel should start to settle into her routine. Healthy cockatiels spend about equal amounts of time during the day eating, playing, sleeping and defecating. You will soon recognize your pet's normal routine. You may also notice that your bird fluffs or shakes her feathers, or that she chirps a greeting when you uncover her cage in the morning.

Don't become alarmed the first time you see your cockatiel asleep. Although it may seem that your bird has lost her head or a leg, she's fine. Sleeping on one foot with her head tucked under her wing (actually with her head turned about 180° and her beak tucked into the feathers on the back of her neck) is a normal sleeping position for many parrots. Be aware, too, that your bird will occasionally perch on one leg while resting the other. Healthy birds do this; an unhealthy bird will not have the strength to balance on leg and foot.

## AMENITIES FOR YOUR COCKATIEL

- a cage
- food and water bowls (at least two sets of each for easier dish changing and cage cleaning)
- perches of varying diameters and materials
- a sturdy scrub brush to clean the perches
- food (a good-quality fresh seed mixture or a formulated diet, such as pellets or crumbles)
- a powdered vitamin and mineral supplement to sprinkle on your pet's fresh foods
- a variety of safe, fun toys
- a cage cover (an old sheet or towel that is free of holes and ravels will serve this purpose nicely)
- a play gym to allow your cockatiel time out of her cage and a place to exercise

13

It is very important to have a radio or television on for your cockatiel if you leave her home alone for long periods of time. In the grasslands of Australia, the cockatiel's first home, silence usually indicates a predator or other danger in the area, which can raise a bird's stress level and may make her more susceptible to illness.

## YOUR COCKATIEL'S HOME

Selecting your cockatiel's cage will be one of the most important decisions you will make for your pet, and where that cage will be located in your home is equally important.

### Choosing a Cage

When selecting a cage for your cockatiel, make sure the bird has room to spread her wings without touching the cage sides. Her tail should not touch the cage bottom, nor should her crest brush the top.

A cage that measures 18×18×24 inches is the minimum size for a single cockatiel, and bigger is always better. If you are planning to keep a pair of birds, the cage should be at least 24×24×40 inches. If your bird must spend a lot of time in her cage, such as all day while you work, select a spacious cage.

Simply put, buy the largest cage designed for cockatiels you can afford because you don't want your pet to feel cramped. Remember, too, that a parrot is like a little airplane flying across an area, rather than a little helicopter that hovers up and down. For this reason, long, rectangular

*A wire cage that's spacious, clean and contains food, water and toys, is a good home for your cockatiel.*

cages that offer horizontal space for short flights are preferred to high, tall cages that don't provide much flying room. Place perches across the width at each end so your bird can fly between them.

Chances are that you'll select a wire cage for your cockatiel. Some cages are sold as part of a cockatiel start-up kit, while others are sold simply as cages. Discuss your options with the salesperson at your local pet supply store. Find out what advantages there are to purchasing a complete kit.

Regardless of whether it's a kit or pre-built, examine any cage you choose carefully before making your final selection. Make sure that the finish is not chipped, bubbled or peeling, because your pet may find the spot and continue removing the finish, which can cause a cage to look old and worn before its time. Also, your pet could become ill if she ingests any of the finish.

Reject any cages that have sharp interior wires or wide bar spacing. (Recommended bar spacing for cockatiels is about $1/2$ inch.) Finally, make sure the cage you choose has some horizontal bars in it so your cockatiel will be able to climb the cage walls easily for exercise.

*A good cage is one that's easy to clean and take food and water in and out of.*

Once you've checked the overall cage quality and the bar spacing, look at the cage door. Does it open easily for you, yet remain secure enough to keep your bird in her cage when you close the door? Is it wide enough for you to get your hand in and out of the cage comfortably? Will your bird's food bowl or a bowl of bath water fit through it easily? Does the door open up, down or to the side? Avoid those that slide up, guillotine style.

Next, look at the cage tray. Does it slide in and out of the cage easily? Remember that you will be changing the paper in this tray at least once a day for the rest of your bird's life (about fifteen years with

*Where you put the cage is important; you want your cock-atiel to feel safe in it.*

good care). Is the tray an odd shape or size? Will paper need to be cut into unusual shapes to fit in it, or will paper towels, newspapers or clean sheets of used computer paper fit easily into it? The easier the tray is to remove and reline, the more likely you will be to change the lining of the tray daily. Can the cage tray be replaced if it becomes damaged and unusable? Ask your pet store staff before making your purchase. It is easy to keep clean? Avoid any that have seams in which food may get caught.

Finally, check the floor of the cage you've chosen. Does it have a grille that will keep your bird out of the debris that falls to the bottom of the cage, such as feces, seed hulls, molted feathers and discarded food? To ensure your pet's long-term health, it's best to have a grille between your curious pet and the remains in the cage tray. It's also easier to keep your cockatiel in her cage while you're cleaning the cage tray if there's a grille between the cage and the tray. A removable grille will be far easier to clean than one that is stationary.

## What to Put in the Cage Tray

It is recommended that you use clean black-and-white newsprint, white paper towels or clean sheets of used computer printer paper. Sand, ground corncobs or walnut shells may be sold by your pet supply store, but are not recommended as cage flooring materials because they tend to hide feces and discarded food quite well. These substrates are also an ideal place for dangerous bacteria to grow.

## CAGE LOCATION

Now that you've picked the perfect cage for your pet, where will you put it? Your cockatiel will be happiest when she's part of the family, so consider the living room, family room or dining room. If your cockatiel is a child's pet, she may do well living in her young owner's room if a child spends a lot of time with her.

Avoid keeping your bird in the bathroom or kitchen, because sudden temperature fluctuations or fumes from cleaning products used in those rooms could harm your pet. Another spot to avoid is a busy hall or entryway, because the activity level and abrupt temperature changes in these spots may be too

17

*Cockatiel owners have lots of cage accessories to choose from!*

much for your pet. Set up the cage so that it is at your eye level if possible, because it will make servicing the cage and visiting with your pet easier for you. It will also reduce the stress on your cockatiel, because birds like to be up high for security.

Regardless of the room you select for your cockatiel, be sure to put the cage in a secure corner (with one solid wall behind the cage to ensure your cockatiel's sense of security). Place non-toxic plants on one side for added security. Please don't put the cage in direct sun, though,

because cockatiels can quickly overheat.

## Cage Accessories

Along with the perfect-size cage in the ideal location in your home, your pet will need a few cage accessories. These include food and water dishes, perches, toys and a cage cover.

### FOOD DISHES

Cockatiels seem to enjoy food crocks; these open ceramic bowls allow the birds to hop up on the edge of the bowl and pick and choose what they will during the day. Be sure to purchase shallow dishes that are less than 1 inch deep.

### PERCHES

When choosing perches for your pet's cage, try to buy at least two different diameters, each made of a different material so your bird's feet won't get tired of standing on the same-sized perch made of the same material day after day.

The recommended diameter for cockatiel perches is $5/8$ inch, so try to buy one perch that's this size and one that is slightly larger ($3/4$ inch, for example). Birds spend almost all

*Perches should be placed so that your cockatiels have different levels to rest on.*

18

of their lives standing, so keeping their feet healthy is important. Also, avian foot problems are much easier to prevent than they are to treat.

You'll probably notice a lot of different kinds of perches when you visit your pet store. Along with the traditional wooden dowels, bird owners can purchase perches made from manzanita branches, cotton rope and terra-cotta or concrete.

Manzanita offers birds varied diameters on the same perch, along with chewing possibilities. Rope perches also offer varied diameter and a softer perching surface than wood or plastic, and terra-cotta and concrete provide slightly abrasive surfaces that birds can use to groom their beaks without severely damaging the skin on their feet in the process. Some bird owners have reported that their pets have suffered foot abrasions with these perches, however; watch your pet carefully for signs of sore feet (an inability to perch or climb, favoring a foot or raw, sore skin on the feet) if you choose to use these perches in your pet's cage. It's best to have only one of these perches in a cage; your pet can then choose where she will sit. Combine one concrete or terra cotta perch with a manzanita perch

*Your cockatiel will appreciate a rope toy, among others.*

19

and (especially important) a cotton rope perch.

Do not use sandpaper covers on her perches. These sleeves, touted as nail-trimming devices, really do little to trim a parrot's nails because birds don't usually drag their nails along their perches. They are good at abrading the surface of your cockatiel's feet; however, this can leave her vulnerable to infections and can make moving and standing painful for your pet.

When placing perches in your bird's cage, try to vary the heights so your bird has different "levels" in her

## HOMEMADE TOYS

Entertaining and safe toys can be made at home. Give your bird an empty paper towel roll or toilet paper tube (from unscented paper only, please), string some Cheerios on a piece of vegetable-tanned leather or offer your bird a dish of raw pasta pieces to destroy. Ladders, swings, perches and toys stimulate your cockatiel's mind and also provide opportunity for exercise.

cage. Don't place any perches over food or water dishes, because birds can and will contaminate food or water by defecating in it or dropping discarded food. Finally, place one perch higher than the rest for a nighttime sleeping roost. Cockatiels and other parrots like to sleep on the highest point they can find to perch.

### Choosing the Right Toys

Cockatiels enjoy the following types of toys: chewable wooden items, ranging from clothes pegs (not clothespins, which have potentially dangerous springs that can snap on a bird's wing or leg) to spools; wooden ladders, sturdy ropes or cords to climb on; bells to ring; knotted rope or leather toys to preen and chew on; and mirrors to admire themselves in. Be warned, though, that if you give a single cockatiel a mirror toy, she may bond to the reflection she sees and consider the bird in the mirror a more interesting companion than you!

Evaluate any toy for safety. Good choices include sturdy wooden toys (either undyed or painted with bird-safe vegetable dye or food coloring) strung on closed-link chains or vegetable-tanned leather thongs and rope toys. If you purchase rope toys for your cockatiel, make sure her nails are trimmed regularly to prevent them from snagging in the rope, and discard the toy when it becomes frayed. All bells should be the open type you might see in a church steeple; avoid the jingle-bell type (round types you often see during the December holidays). Your pet could catch her toenails or toe in one of the small holes or slits and sustain a serious injury.

Unsafe items to watch out for are brittle plastic toys that can be shattered easily by a cockatiel's beak,

*This cockatiel is enjoying some time outside her cage exercising on her play gym.*

lead-weighted toys that can be cracked open to expose the dangerous lead to curious birds, loose-link chains that can catch toenails or beaks, ring toys that are too small to climb through safely.

## The Cage Cover

One important, but sometimes overlooked, accessory is the cage cover. Be sure that you have something to cover your cockatiel's cage with when it's time to put your pet to sleep each night. The act of covering the cage seems to calm many pet birds and convince them that it's really time to go to bed despite the sounds of an active family evening in the background.

You can purchase a cage cover, or you can use an old sheet, blanket or towel that is clean and free of holes. Be aware that some birds like to chew on their cage covers through the cage bars. If your bird does this, replace the cover when it becomes too tattered to do its job effectively. A night light can also help your pet's night fears.

## The Play Gym

Although your cockatiel will spend quite a bit of time in her cage, she will also need time out of her cage to exercise and to enjoy a change of scenery. A play gym can help keep your pet physically and mentally active.

If you visit a large pet store or bird specialty store, or if you look through the pages of any pet bird hobbyist magazine, you will see a variety of play gyms on display. You can choose a complicated gym with a series of ladders, swings, perches and toys, or you can purchase a simple T-stand that has a place for food and water bowls and a screw or two from which you can hang toys. If you're really handy with tools, you can even construct a gym to your cockatiel's specifications.

# CHAPTER THREE

# Cockatiel Particulars

M ost new bird owners have high expectations for developing a loving relationship with their pet. The goal is to nurture a relationship with your cockatiel that will result in a bird who will interact well with people, be pleasant company and show little sign of aggressiveness (such as screaming).

## BASIC COCKATIEL BEHAVIOR

The following common avian behaviors are listed in alphabetical order to help you better understand your new feathered friend!

## *Attention-Getting Behaviors*

As your cockatiel becomes more settled in your home, don't be surprised if you hear subtle little fluffs coming from under the cage cover first thing in the morning. It's as if your bird is saying, "I hear that you're up. I'm up, too. Don't forget to uncover me and play with me!" Other attention-getting behaviors include gently shaking toys, sneezing or soft vocalizations.

## Beak Grinding

If you hear your bird making odd little grinding noises as he's drifting off to sleep, don't be alarmed! Beak grinding is a sign of a contented pet bird.

## Beak Wiping

After a meal, a cockatiel will wipe his beak against a perch, the cage bars or on the cage floor to clean it.

## Birdie Aerobics

This is a sudden bout of stretching that all parrots seem to do. An otherwise calm bird will suddenly grab the cage bars and stretch the wing and leg muscles on one side of his body, or he will raise both wings in imitation of an eagle.

## Tail Flipping

A contented cockatiel may flip his tail back and forth. This usually happens after a satisfying bath, stretching activity or play session with you.

*Cockatiels will often raise both wings to stretch in a form of birdie aerobics.*

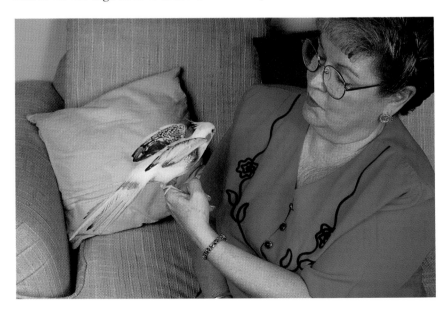

## Catnaps

You will probably catch your cockatiel taking a little catnap during the day. These active little birds seem to be either going full-tilt, playing and eating, or catching a few Zs. As long as you see no other indications of illness, such as a loss of appetite or fluffed feathers in a warm house, there is no need to worry if your pet sleeps during the day, especially if he sits on one foot at least part of the resting time.

## Feather Picking

Don't confuse this with preening (see below). Feather picking results from physical causes, such as a dietary imbalance, a hormonal change, a thyroid problem or an infection of the skin or feathers. It can also be caused by emotional upset, such as a change in the bird's routine, a new baby in the home or a number of other factors. Once feather picking begins, it may be difficult to get a bird to stop. If you notice that your bird suddenly starts pulling his feathers out, contact your avian veterinarian for an evaluation.

## Fluffing

This is often a prelude to preening or a tension releaser. If your bird fluffs up and stays fluffed, however, contact your avian veterinarian for an appointment because fluffed feathers can be an indicator of illness.

## Hissing

If your cockatiel hisses, it's because he is frightened of something in his environment that he's trying to scare away by hissing.

## Mutual Preening

This can take place between birds or between birds and their owners. It is a sign of affection reserved for best friends or mates, so consider it an honor if your cockatiel wants to preen your eyebrows, hair, mustache or beard, or the hair on your arms and hands.

## Pair Bonding

This is discussed in the context of breeding later in the book, but I wanted to include it here, too, to point out that not only mated pairs bond. But best bird buddies of the same sex will demonstrate some of the same behavior, including sitting close to each other, preening each other and mimicking the other's actions, such as stretching or scratching and mutual preening or grooming.

## Possessiveness

Cockatiels can become overly attached to one person in the household, especially if that person is primarily responsible for his care. Indications of a possessive cockatiel can include hissing and other threatening gestures made toward other family members, and pair bonding behavior with the chosen family member.

You can keep your cockatiel from becoming possessive by having all members of the family spend time with the bird from the time you first bring him home. Encourage different members of the family to feed the bird and clean his cage, and make sure all family members play with the bird and socialize him while he's out of his cage.

## Preening

This is part of a cockatiel's normal routine. You will see your bird ruffling and straightening his feathers each day. He will also take oil from the uropygial or preen gland on his back at the base of his tail and put the oil on the rest of his feathers, so don't be concerned if you see your pet seeming to peck or bite at his tail. If, during molting, your bird seems to remove whole feathers, don't panic!

## Regurgitating

If you see your bird pinning his eyes (pupils enlarge, then contract, then enlarge again), bobbing his head and pumping his neck and crop muscles, he is about to regurgitate some food for you. Birds regurgitate to their mates during breeding season and to their young chicks. It is a mark of great affection to have your bird regurgitate his dinner for you, so try not to be too disgusted!

## Resting on One Foot

Do not be alarmed if you see your cockatiel occasionally resting on only one foot. This is normal behavior (the resting foot is often drawn up into the belly feathers). If you see your bird always using both feet to perch, please contact your avian veterinarian because this can indicate a health problem.

## Screaming

Well-cared-for cockatiels will vocalize quietly (see separate entry for vocalization), but birds that feel neglected and that have little attention paid to them may become screamers. Screaming can be a difficult habit to break, particularly if the bird feels rewarded with your negative attention every time he screams. You may not see your attention as a reward, but at least the bird gets to see you and to hear from you as you tell him (often in a loud, dramatic way) to be quiet.

Remember to give your bird consistent attention (at least thirty minutes a day); provide him with an interesting environment, complete with a variety of toys, a well-balanced diet; and leave a radio or television on when you're away to provide background noise. These measures can help to prevent your

bird from becoming a habitual screamer.

## Sneezing

In pet birds, sneezes are classified as either nonproductive or productive. Nonproductive sneezes clear a bird's nares (what we think of as nostrils) and are nothing to worry about. Some birds even stick a claw into their nares which induces a sneeze from time to time. If your bird sneezes frequently and you see a discharge from his nares or notice the area around his nares is wet, contact your avian veterinarian immediately to set up an appointment to have your bird's health checked.

*This cockatiel is preening himself with abandon!*

## LEARN TO READ A COCKATIEL'S MOOD BY ITS CREST

Here's what to look for:

- Content cockatiels keep their crests lowered. Only the tips of the feathers point upward.

- Playful, alert cockatiels raise their crests vertically. This position indicates that the bird is ready for action.

- Agitated cockatiels raise their crests straight up and have the feather tips leaning forward slightly.

- Frightened cockatiels whip their crests back and hiss in a threatening manner. They also stand tall, ready to fight or take flight as the situation dictates. A playful cockatiel will have an alert, inquisitive demeanor. It is natural and healthy for your cockatiel to display aggressive behavior if he senses a threat. Make sure that the room your cockatiel is exploring has been "bird-proofed" for safety.

### Stress

This can show itself in many ways in your bird's behavior, including shaking, diarrhea, rapid breathing, wing and tail fanning, screaming, feather picking, poor sleeping habits or loss of appetite. Over a period of time, stress can harm your cockatiel's health. To prevent your bird from becoming stressed, try to provide him with as normal and regular a routine as possible. Parrots are, for the most part, creatures of habit, and they don't always adapt well to sudden changes in their environment or schedule.

### Tasting/Testing Things with the Beak

Birds use their beaks and tongues to explore their world in much the same way people use their hands. For example, don't be surprised if your cockatiel reaches out to gently taste or bite your hand before stepping onto it the first time. Your bird isn't biting you to be mean; he's merely investigating his world and testing the strength of a new "perch."

### Thrashing

Cockatiels, particularly lutinos, seem prone to a condition that is described as "night frights," "cockatiel thrashing syndrome" or "earthquake syndrome." Birds that have thrashing episodes will be startled

28

*Cockatiels use their beaks and feet to explore their world, but especially their beaks.*

29

from sleep by loud noises or vibrations that might cause a wild bird to awaken suddenly and try to take flight. In the case of caged pet birds, the thrasher may injure his wing tips, feet, chest or abdomen on toys or cage bars when he tries to flee from the perceived danger. The next morning you might find a frightened bird and blood splattered on the nearby wall.

Bird owners can help protect their pets from harm by installing a small night-light near the bird's cage to help the bird see where he is during a thrashing episode, by placing an air cleaner in the bird's room to provide "white noise" that will drown out some potentially frightening background noises or by placing the bird in a small sleeping cage that is free of toys and other items that could harm a frightened bird.

## Threats

If your cockatiel wants to threaten a cagemate, another pet in the home or one of his human companions, he will stand as tall as he can with his crest raised halfway and his mouth open. He will also try to bite the object of his threats.

## TOXIC HOUSEPLANTS

This list may not include all potentially dangerous plants. Before you put any plants in reach of your bird, please check a garden book for plants toxic to children. If you are unsure, err on the cautious side and keep the plant away from your bird. Better yet, don't buy it.

- amaryllis
- bird of paradise
- calla lily
- daffodil
- dieffenbachia
- English ivy
- foxglove
- holly
- juniper
- lily-of-the-valley
- mistletoe
- oleander
- philodendron
- rhododendron
- rhubarb
- sweet pea
- wisteria

### *Vocalization*

Many parrots vocalize around sunrise and sunset, which I believe hearkens back to flock behavior in the wild when parrots call to each other to start and end their days. You may notice that your pet cockatiel calls to you when you are out of the room. This may mean that he feels lonely or that he needs some

reassurance from you. Tell him that he's fine and that he's being a good bird, and the bird should settle down and begin playing or eating. If he continues to call to you, however, you may want to check on him to ensure that everything is all right in his world.

## HOUSEHOLD HAZARDS

The phrase "curiosity killed the cat" could easily be rewritten to reflect a cockatiel's curious nature. These inquisitive little birds seem to be able to get into just about anything, which means they can get themselves into potentially dangerous situations rather quickly. Because of this natural curiosity, cockatiel owners must be extremely vigilant when their birds are out of their cages.

Part of this vigilance should include bird-proofing your home. Remember that some of the larger parrots are intellectually on a similar level as a toddler. You wouldn't let a toddler have free run of your house without taking a few precautions to safeguard the child from harm, and you should extend the same concern to your pet birds.

Let's go room by room and look at some of the potentially dangerous situations you should be aware of.

## Bathroom

This can be a cockatiel paradise if the bird is allowed to spend time with you as you prepare for work or for an evening out, but it can also be quite harmful to your bird's health. An open toilet could lead to the cockatiel drowning, the bird could hurt himself chewing on the cord of your blow-dryer or he could be overcome by fumes from perfume, hairspray, medications or cleaning products. Use caution when taking your bird into the bathroom, and make sure his wings are clipped to avoid flying accidents.

## Kitchen

This is another popular spot for birds and their owners to hang out, especially around mealtime. Here again, dangers lurk for curious cockatiels. An unsupervised bird could fly or fall into the trash can, or he could climb into the oven, dishwasher, freezer or refrigerator and be forgotten. Your bird could also land on a hot stove or fall into an uncovered pot of boiling water. The bird could also become poisoned by eating foods that are unsafe for him,

*A ceiling fan makes a great perch for a curious cockatiel, but can pose a grave danger if turned on.*

## SAFE HOUSEPLANTS

- African violets
- aloe
- burro's tail
- Christmas cactus
- coleus
- edible fig
- gardenia
- grape ivy
- fern (asparagus, Boston, bird's nest, maidenhair, ribbon, staghorn, squirrel's foot)

- hens and chickens
- hibiscus
- jade plant
- kalanchoe
- pepperomia
- rubber plant
- spider plant
- yucca
- palms (butterfly, cane, golden feather, Madagascar, European fan, sentry and pygmy date)

such as chocolate, avocado or rhubarb.

## Living Room

Are you sitting on your couch or in a comfortable chair as you read this book? Although it probably seems safe enough to you, your pet could be injured or killed if he decided to play hide-and-seek under pillows or cushions and was accidentally sat on. The space under a recliner may also tempt your bird,

but if someone sits in the chair or sits forward, snapping the foot rest to the base of the chair, the bird could be seriously injured or killed. Your cockatiel could become poisoned by nibbling on a leaded glass lampshade or the leaded weights in the bottom of drapes, or he could fly out an open window or patio door. By the same token, he could fly into a closed window or door and injure himself severely. He could become entangled in a drapery cord or a venetian blind pull, he could fall into an uncovered fish tank and drown or he could ingest poison by nibbling on ashes or used cigarette butts in an ashtray.

## Home Office

This can be another cockatiel playground, but you'll have to be on your toes to keep your pet from harming himself by nibbling on potentially poisonous markers, glue sticks or crayons.

## Other Areas of Concern

If you have a ceiling fan in your house, make sure it is turned off when your bird is out of his cage. Make sure you know where your bird is before turning on your washer or dryer, and don't close your basement freezer without checking first to be sure your bird isn't in there.

This doesn't mean to keep your bird locked up in his cage all the time. On the contrary, all parrots need as much time as possible out of their cages to maintain physical and mental health. The key is to be aware of some of the dangers that may exist in your home and to pay attention to your bird's behavior so you can intervene before the bird becomes ill or injured.

Unfortunately, potential dangers to a pet bird don't stop with the furniture and accessories. A variety of fumes can overpower your cockatiel.

To help protect your pet from harmful chemical fumes, consider using some "green" cleaning alternatives, such as baking soda and vinegar to clear clogged drains, baking soda instead of scouring powder to clean tubs and sinks, half of a lemon ground in your disposer to remove odors, lemon juice and mineral oil to polish furniture and white vinegar and water as a window cleaner.

If you're considering a remodeling or home improvement project, think about your cockatiel first. Fumes from paint or formaldehyde,

*Pets fill important roles in our lives and our families.*

*Cockatiels are sociable birds and, with gentle handling, enjoy being with people.*

34

which can be found in carpet backing, paneling and particle board, can cause pets and people to become ill. If you are having work done on your home, consider boarding your cockatiel at your avian veterinarian's office or at the home of a bird-loving friend or relative until the project is complete and the house is aired out. If your house must be treated chemically, arrange to board your bird at your avian veterinarian's office or with a friend before, during and after the fumigation to ensure that no harm comes to your pet. Make sure your house is aired out completely before bringing your bird home, too. If you suspect that your

cockatiel ingested something toxic, contact the National Animal Poison Control Hotline (800) 548-2423.

## Other Pets

Other pets can harm your cockatiel's health, too. A curious cat could claw or bite your pet, a dog could step on him accidentally or bite him, or another, larger bird could break his leg or rip off his upper mandible. If your cockatiel tangles with another pet in your home, contact your avian veterinarian immediately because emergency treatment (for bacterial infection from a puncture wound or shock from being stepped on or suffering a broken bone) may be required to save your bird's life.

## CARING FOR OLDER BIRDS

If you've offered your cockatiel a varied, healthy diet, taken him to the vet regularly, clipped his wings faithfully and kept his environment clean and interesting, chances are your bird will live into old age. You may notice subtle changes in your bird's appearance and habits as he ages. He may molt more erratically and his feathers may grow in more sparsely as he ages, or he may seem to preen himself less often.

Although little is known about the nutritional requirements of older pet birds, avian veterinarians Branson W. Ritchie and Greg J. Harrison suggest in their book Avian *Medicine: Principles and Applications* (co-authored with Linda R. Harrison) that older pet birds should eat a highly digestible diet that allows a bird to maintain her weight while receiving lower levels of proteins, phosphorus and sodium. They also suggest that this diet contain slightly higher levels of vitamins A, E, B12, thiamin, pridoxine, zinc, linoleic acid and lysine may help birds cope with the metabolic and digestive changes that come with old age.

## When Your Bird Dies

Although birds are relatively long-lived pets, eventually the wonderful relationship between bird and owner ends when the bird dies. While no one has an easy time accepting the death of a beloved pet, children may have more difficulty with the loss than adults. To help your child cope, consider the following suggestions:

Let your child know that it's okay to feel sad about losing your cockatiel. Encourage your child to draw pictures of the bird, to make a collage using photos of your pet or pictures of cockatiels from magazines, to write stories or poems about him or to talk about your loss. Also explain to the child that these sad feelings will pass with time. Regardless of a child's age, being honest about the loss of your bird is the best approach to help all family members cope with the loss.

While helping their children cope with the death of a pet, parents need to remember that it's okay for adults to feel sad, too. Don't diminish your feelings of loss by saying

35

*This senior bird is happy and healthy.*

"It's only a bird." Pets fill important roles in our lives and our families. Whenever we lose someone close to us, we grieve.

Although you may feel as though you never want another bird because of the pain caused by your bird's death, don't let the loss of your cockatiel keep you from owning other birds. While you can never replace your cockatiel completely, you may find that you miss having a feathered companion around your house. Some people will want a new pet bird almost immediately after suffering a loss, while others will want to wait a few weeks or months before bringing another bird home. Maybe you want another cockatiel, or perhaps you'd like to try owning a different avian species. Discuss bringing home a new pet bird with your family, your avian veterinarian and bird breeders in your area.

## IF YOUR BIRD FLIES AWAY . . .

One of the most common accidents that befalls bird owners is that a fully flighted bird escapes through an open door or window. Cockatiel owners are at particular risk to lose their birds because cockatiels are so aerodynamic and such strong fliers. Just because your bird has never flown before or shown any interest in leaving his cage doesn't mean that he can't fly or that he won't become disoriented once he's outside. If you don't believe it can happen, just check the lost and found advertisements in your local newspaper for a week. Chances are many more cockatiels turn up in the "lost" column than in the "found" one.

Why do lost birds never come home? Some birds fall victim to predatory animals in the wild, while others join flocks of feral, or wild, parrots. Still other lost birds end up so far away from home because they fly wildly and frantically in any direction that the people who find them don't advertise in the same area that the birds were lost in. Finally, some people who find lost birds don't advertise that they've been found because the finders think that whoever was unlucky or uncaring enough to lose the bird in the first place doesn't deserve to have him back.

## Prevention

How can you prevent your bird from becoming lost? First, make sure his wings are safely trimmed at regular intervals. Be sure to trim both wings evenly and remember to trim wings after your bird has molted.

Next, be sure your bird's cage door locks securely and that his cage tray cannot come loose if the cage is knocked over or dropped accidentally. Also be sure that all your window screens fit securely and are free from tears and large holes. Keep all window screens and patio doors closed when your bird is at liberty. Finally, don't ever go outside with your bird on your shoulder.

If, despite your best efforts, your bird should escape, you must act quickly for the best chance of recovering your pet.

## TAMING YOUR COCKATIEL

If you have acquired a hand-fed cockatiel, chances are that the breeder spent time each day working with your bird to tame it. If your bird was not tamed before you acquired him, you will have to begin

## IF YOUR COCKATIEL TAKES FLIGHT . . .

- Have an audiotape of your bird's voice and a portable tape recorder available to lure your bird back home.

- Place your bird's cage in an area where your bird is likely to see it, such as on a deck or patio. Put lots of treats and food on the floor of the cage to tempt your pet back into his home.

- Use another caged bird to attract your cockatiel's attention.

- Alert your avian veterinarian's office that your bird has escaped. Also let the local humane society and other veterinary offices in your area know.

- Post fliers in your neighborhood describing your bird. Offer a reward and include your phone number.

37

the taming process by gaining your pet's trust, and then working to never lose it. You must also be sure not to lose your temper with your bird and never hit him, even if the bird makes you very angry. If your bird destroyed something, you were at fault for failing to remove off-limits objects.

Although parrots are clever creatures, they are not "cause and effect" thinkers. If your cockatiel chews on a picture frame on your end table, he won't associate you yelling at him or locking him in his cage with the original misbehavior. As a result, most traditional forms of discipline are ineffective with parrots.

## Gentle Discipline

So what do you do when your cockatiel misbehaves? When you must discipline your pet, look at him sternly (what bird behaviorist Sally Blanchard calls "the evil eye") and tell him "No" in a firm voice. If the bird is climbing on or chewing something he shouldn't, also remove him from the source as you tell him "No." If your bird has become a screaming banshee, sometimes a little "time out" in his covered cage (between five and ten minutes in most cases) does wonders to calm him down.

If your cockatiel bites you while he's perched on your hand or if he begins chewing on your clothing or jewelry, you can often dissuade him from this behavior by rotating your

*Teach your cockatiel to step onto your finger to come out of the cage.*

wrist about a quarter turn to simulate a small "earthquake." Your cockatiel will quickly associate the rocking of his "perch" with his misbehavior and will stop biting or chewing.

## Building Trust

A good first step in building trust with your cockatiel is getting him comfortable around you. Give your bird a bit of warning before you approach his cage. Call his name when you walk into the room. Move slowly around your pet. These gestures will help him become more comfortable with you. Reassure the bird that everything is all right and that he's a wonderful pet.

After your bird is comfortable having you in the same room with him, try placing your hand in his cage and holding it there for a few seconds. Don't be surprised if your bird flutters around and squawks at first at the "intruder."

Continue this process daily, and leave your hand in the cage for slightly longer periods of time each day. Within a few days, your bird won't make a fuss about your hand being in his space, and he may come over to investigate this new perch.

## TRAINING TIPS

- Provide a safe and secure training environment.

- Respect your cockatiel's likes and dislikes.

- Keep sessions short and fun.

- Praise and reward every effort. Keep your arm as stable as possible to help your cockatiel feel safe.

Do not remove your hand from the cage the first time your cockatiel lands on it; just let the bird become accustomed to perching on your hand.

After several successful perching attempts on successive days, try to take your hand out of the cage with your bird on it. Some cockatiels will take to this new adventure willingly, while others are reluctant to leave the safety and security of home.

Once your cockatiel is willing to come out of his cage on your hand, see if you can make perching on your hand a game for your pet. Once he masters perching on your hand, you can teach him to step up by gently pressing your finger up and into the bird's belly. This will cause the bird to step up. As he

39

*While training your cockatiel, feed his favorite treats as reinforcement for good behavior.*

does so, say "Step up" or "Up." Before long, your bird will respond to this command without much prompting.

Along with the "Up" command, you may want to teach your cockatiel the "Down" command. When you put the bird down on his cage or play gym, simply say "Down" as the bird steps off your hand. These two simple commands offer a great deal of control for you over your bird, because you can say "Up" to put an unruly bird back in his cage or you can tell a parrot that needs to

go to bed "Down" as you put the bird in his cage at night.

After your pet has become comfortable sitting on your hand, try petting him. Birds seem to like to have their heads, backs, cheek patches, under wing areas and eye areas (including the closed eyelids) scratched or petted lightly. Quite a few like to have a spot low on their backs at the bases of their tails (over their preen glands) rubbed. Many birds do not enjoy having their stomachs scratched, although yours may think this is heaven! You'll have to experiment to see where your bird likes to be petted. You'll know you're successful if your bird clicks or grinds his beak, pins its eyes or settles onto your hand or into your lap with a completely relaxed, blissful expression on his face.

# TRICKS!

Trick training a cockatiel may seem like a daunting task, but it really isn't. You've already trained your pet to perform simple tricks when he learns the "Up" and "Down" with your fingers. You can make further trick training easier by first watching your bird and seeing what he's naturally inclined to do. For example, does your bird spend a lot of time climbing on his ladder or on his rope toys? If he does, make climbing an important part of any tricks you teach your pet. If your bird raises his wings frequently, it may be a good candidate to learn how to salute or "be an eagle." When he does so, say "be an eagle," and then reward him.

Birds less than 6 months of age seem to be easier to teach tricks to than adult cockatiels, and inexperienced trainers may find greater success with younger birds.

Patience on your part and a cheerful demeanor and attitude will go a long way toward making the training sessions more pleasant for both you and your pet. Your patience will be rewarded by a more enjoyable relationship with your pet bird.

## Positive Reinforcement

Another key to trick training success is to use positive reinforcement to reward your bird's good behavior. Bird trainer Steve Martin further breaks down positive reinforcement into primary reinforcers, such as a favorite treat, and secondary reinforcers, such as praise or a scratch on the head. When you first begin training your cockatiel, primary reinforcers will be the reward you want to use. As your bird learns and perfects a trick, you can use secondary reinforcers to reward his behavior.

Some people would tell you that in order to train your bird successfully, you should withhold food from him so that he's hungry. Think how you feel when you're hungry? Do you concentrate well and want to learn new things quickly? I'd imagine that you don't, and your bird is

## A QUICK TRICK

An easy trick to teach your cockatiel is to shake his head "yes" or "no" as if he's agreeing or disagreeing with you. To do this, show your bird a treat and move it up and down in front of your bird's face to teach him "yes" and from side to side to teach him "no." Praise the bird when he moves his head in the proper direction and give him the treat. Use a phrase like "Do you agree?" as a command or cue when training your bird to nod his head "yes." As you teach this trick, move the treat a little bit further away from your bird with each repetition and wait a bit longer to praise and reward your cockatiel with his treat. Finally, don't teach these tricks simultaneously because you might confuse the cockatiel.

Before you know it, you'll be amazing your friends and family with your trick-trained bird! If, however, your pet doesn't seem to enjoy the training sessions, don't force him into becoming a performer. Instead, appreciate him for the wonderful creature that he is.

no different. To reward your cockatiel's good behavior, follow trainer Steve Martin's advice and pick one favorite treat, such as half a peanut or a sunflower seed. Use this treat as a reward only during your training sessions and eliminate it from your bird's diet otherwise. In this way, you've modified your bird's diet somewhat to make the treat a special reward without depriving it of food completely.

The treat can also help you gauge the length of a training session. When your bird has lost interest in this favored treat, end the training session; your bird's lack of interest means you've probably lost his attention for learning the trick as well. If possible, try to end the session before your bird loses interest in the treat.

## *How to Get Started*

To start trick training your cockatiel, praise him and reward him with a treat when you see the bird doing something—lifting his wing, for instance—that could translate into a trick later on. Your bird will soon associate his actions with attention and positive reinforcement from you, which will make him all the more likely to perform the behavior in the future. Reinforce the behavior with praise and a treat every time you see your bird perform it.

After a few sessions of praising the chosen behavior, you should have your bird accustomed to receiving praise for a particular action.

Now you can devise a command to prompt the bird into performing the behavior. For example, if you've praised that winglifting bird for raising his wing, you can now cue the bird to "salute." Once you've settled on an appropriate command, praise the bird *only* when he follows your directions. If he doesn't follow your command, don't punish him. Instead, ask him to perform the trick again and praise him when him follows your instructions.

# CHAPTER FOUR

# Positively Nutritious

Although they live in arid climates, wild cockatiels spend a great deal of their time foraging for ripening grass seeds, which are high in carbohydrates and lower in proteins and fats. This need for sprouted fresh foods makes a simple seed-and-water diet unsuitable for pet birds. Poor diet also causes a number of health problems (respiratory infections, poor feather condition, flaky skin, reproductive problems, to name a few) and is one of the main reasons some cockatiels live fairly short lives.

## NUTRITION REQUIREMENTS

According to avian veterinarian Gary Gallerstein, birds require about a dozen vitamins—A, D, E, K, $B_1$, $B_2$, niacin, $B_6$, $B_{12}$, pantothenic acid, biotin, folic acid and choline—to stay healthy, but they can only partially manufacture $D_3$ and niacin. A balanced diet can help provide the rest. To meet these requirements, offer your bird fresh whole fruits and vegetables in addition to her seeds or seeds and pellets.

Along with the vitamins listed above, pet birds need trace amounts of some minerals to maintain good health. These minerals are calcium, phosphorus, sodium, chlorine, potassium, magnesium, iron, zinc, copper, sulphur, iodine and manganese. These can be provided with a well-balanced diet and a supplemental mineral block or cuttlebone. Carrots, for example, are rich in calcium.

Ideally, your cockatiel's diet should contain about equal parts of seed, grain and legumes and dark green or dark orange vegetables and fruits. You can supplement these with small amounts of well-cooked meat or eggs, or calcium-rich vegetables. Let's look at each part of this diet in a little more detail.

## Seeds

First, the seeds, grains and legumes portion of your bird's diet can include clean, fresh seed from your local pet supply store. Try to buy your birdseed from a store where stock turns over quickly. The dusty box on the bottom shelf of a store with little traffic isn't as nutritious for your pet as a bulk purchase of seeds from a freshly filled bin in a busy shop. When you bring the

seeds home, refrigerate them to keep them from becoming "buggy."

To ensure your bird is receiving the proper nutrients from her diet, you need to know if the seed you're serving is fresh. One way to do this is to try sprouting some of the seeds. (Sprouted seeds can also tempt a finicky eater to broaden her diet.)

To sprout seeds, you will need to soak them overnight in lukewarm water. Drain the water off and let the seeds sit in a closed cupboard or other out-of-the-way place for twenty-four hours. Rinse the sprouted seeds thoroughly before offering them to your bird. If the seeds don't sprout, they aren't fresh, and you'll need to find another source for your bird's food.

*Provide your cockatiel with plenty of fresh seeds in her dish.*

45

*Besides fresh seeds, make sure you feed your cockatiel a variety of fruits and vegetables.*

Be sure, too, that your pet has an adequate supply of seeds in its dish at all times. Some cockatiels are such neat eaters that they drop the empty seed hulls back into their dishes. This seemingly full dish can lead to a very hungry cockatiel if an owner isn't observant enough to check the dish carefully. Rather than just looking in the dish while it's in the cage, I suggest that you take the dish out and inspect it over the trash can so you can empty the seed hulls and refill the dish easily. An easy way to do this is to blow on the seeds gently. The hulls are light, and this will leave the heavier seeds in the dish; of course, you should do this outside. Better still, discard the seeds left in the dish or

put it outside for wild birds and squirrels.

## MILLET

One foodstuff that is very popular with cockatiels is millet, especially millet sprays. These golden sprays are part treat and part toy. Offer your cockatiel this treat sparingly, however, because it is high in fat! Other items in the bread group that you can offer your pet include unsweetened breakfast cereals, whole wheat bread, cooked beans, cooked rice and pasta.

## Fruits and Vegetables

Dark green or dark orange vegetables and fruits contain vitamin A, which is an important part of a bird's diet and which is missing from the seeds, grains and legumes group. This vitamin helps fight off infection and keeps a bird's eyes, mouth and respiratory system healthy. Some vitamin-A–rich foods are carrots, yams, sweet potatoes, broccoli, dried red peppers, dandelion greens and spinach.

You may be wondering whether or not to offer frozen or canned vegetables and fruits to your bird. Some birds will eat frozen vegetables and fruits, while others turn their beaks up at the somewhat mushy texture of these foodstuffs. The high sodium content in some canned foods may make them unhealthy for your cockatiel. Frozen and canned foods will serve your bird's needs in an emergency, but I would offer only fresh foods on a regular basis.

## OTHER FRESH FOODS

Along with small portions of well-cooked meat, you can also offer your bird bits of tofu, water-packed tuna, fully cooked scrambled eggs. Avoid dairy products, though, because a bird's digestive system lacks the enzyme lactase, which means she cannot process dairy foods.

47

*A varied diet is the healthiest kind for your cockatiel.*

## VITAL VITAMINS AND MINERALS

The foundation for a healthy cockatiel starts with a balanced diet supplemented by vitamins (A, D, E, K, $B_1$, $B_2$, niacin, $B_6$, $B_{12}$, pantothenic acid, biotin, folic acid and choline) as well as minerals (calcium, phosphorus, sodium, chlorine, potassium, magnesium, iron, zinc, copper, sulphur, iodine and manganese). A mineral block or cuttlebone will supplement a well-rounded diet. The seed mixture you feed your cockatiel should be fresh and kept refrigerated until served. Fresh fruits and vegetables supply vitamin A, which prevents infection and promotes respiratory health.

Introduce young cockatiels to healthy people food early so that they learn to appreciate a varied diet. Some adult birds cling tenaciously to seed-only diets, which aren't as healthy for them in the long term. Offer adult birds fresh foods, too, in the hope that they may try something new. Continue to offer these foods. It may take months or years for an adult bird to learn to trust a new food. Eat the food in the bird's presence. Eventually, your pet will try the food and learn to eat it whenever its offered.

Whatever healthy fresh foods you offer your pet, be sure to remove food from the cage promptly to prevent spoilage and to help keep your bird healthy.

## SUPPLEMENTS

You may also be concerned whether your bird is receiving adequate amounts of vitamins and minerals in her diet. If your cockatiel eats daily, she will have no need for vitamin supplements, which can alter the taste and appearance of food. Vitamin-enriched seed diets may provide some supplementation, but some manufacturers add the vitamins and minerals to the seed hull, which your pet will discard while she eats. Avoid adding vitamin and mineral supplements to your bird's water dish, because they can act as a growth medium for bacteria. They may also cause the water to taste different to your bird, which may discourage her from drinking.

### Water

Along with providing fresh food at least twice a day, you need to provide your cockatiel with fresh, clean water twice a day to maintain her

48

good health. One technique is to give fresh water in the morning with vegetables and fruit and to replace the water from the morning that evening when you remove the perishable foods and replace them with seeds or pellets. The water cups tend to build up a dirty film, so take care to cleanse and rinse them thoroughly.

## FOODS TO AVOID

Now that we've looked at foods that are good for your bird, let's look briefly at those that aren't healthful for your pet. These include alcohol,

### INGREDIENTS FOR A HEALTHY COCKATIEL DIET

- Seed mix
- Pellets
- Fresh vegetables
- Fruits in smaller amounts
- Vitamin supplements
- Occasional treats

rhubarb, avocado (the skin and the area around the pit can be toxic), as well as highly salted, sweetened or

*You may enjoy sharing food with your cockatiel.*

## SPROUTING

Serving sprouts is a simple and nutritious way to expand your cockatiel's diet. Sprouted seeds are packed with vitamins and are a tasty addition to the diet. All you need is a sprouting jar, some mesh cloth and a variety of seeds, such as sunflower, mung or radish.

The first step in the technique is to wash and soak the seeds. The seeds should then be kept in a warm location to encourage sprouting. It is important that all of the material used is washed well to avoid spoiling. It takes about two to three days for the seeds to sprout. Once they have sprouted, offer them to your cockatiel for a nutritious treat.

fatty foods. You should especially avoid chocolate because it contains a chemical, theobromine that can kill your cockatiel; so resist the temptation to share this snack with your pet. Also avoid giving your bird seeds or pits from apples, apricots, cherries, peaches, pears and plums because they contain toxic chemicals.

Let common sense be your guide in choosing which foods can be offered to your bird: If it's healthful for you, it's probably okay to share.

While sharing healthy people food with your bird is completely acceptable, sharing something that you've already taken a bite of is not. Human saliva has bacteria that are potentially toxic to birds, so please don't share partially eaten food with your pet. For your bird's health and your peace of mind, get her own portion or plate.

By the same token, please don't kiss your cockatiel on the beak (kiss her on top of her little head instead) or allow your bird to put her head into your mouth, nibble on your lips or preen your teeth. Although you may see birds doing this on television or in magazine pictures, it's really unsafe for your bird's health and well-being.

Along with providing nutrition for your cockatiel, food can serve as a mental diversion. Like their larger cousins the cockatoos, a cockatiel's nimble brain needs challenges throughout the day to keep her from becoming bored.

# THE PELLETED DIET OPTION

In the early 1980s, researchers at the University of California, Davis, began conducting nutritional research on cockatiels to determine what the best diet for pet birds would be. In order to make fair comparisons of the different nutrients, the researchers created formulated diets for the test flock. Avian nutritionists have used the data gleaned from this test flock in creating many of the pelleted diets that are available today.

Pelleted diets are created by mixing as many as forty different nutrients into a mash and then forcing (or extruding) the hot mixture through a machine to form various shapes. Some pelleted diets have colors and flavors added, while others are fairly plain. We do not recommend that you feed your bird exclusively on pellets.

These formulated diets provide more balanced nutrition in an easy-to-serve form that reduces the amount of wasted food and eliminates the chance for a bird to pick through a smorgasbord of healthy foods to find her favorites and reject the foods she isn't particularly fond of. Some cockatiels accept pelleted diets quickly, while others require some persuading.

Whatever you do, don't starve your bird into trying a new food. Offer new foods along with familiar favorites. This will ensure that your bird is eating and will also encourage her to try new foods.

# CHAPTER FIVE

# Pretty Birdie

Your cockatiel has several grooming needs. First, he must be able to bathe regularly, and he will need to have his nails and flight feathers trimmed periodically to ensure his safety.

A healthy bird will not need to have his beak trimmed. If your bird's beak becomes overgrown, please consult your avian veterinarian. A parrot's beak contains a surprising number of blood vessels, so beak trimming is best left to the experts. Also, a suddenly overgrown beak may indicate that your bird is suffering from liver damage, a virus or scaly mites, all of which require veterinary care.

## BATHING

You can bathe your bird in a variety of ways. You can mist him lightly with a clean spray bottle filled with warm water only, you can allow him to bathe in the kitchen or bathroom sink under a slow stream of water or you can take him into the shower with you. Bathing is important to birds to help them keep their feathers clean and healthy, so don't deny your pet the chance to bathe!

Unless your cockatiel has gotten himself into oil, paint, wax or some other substance that elbow grease alone won't remove and that could harm his feathers, he will not require soap as part of his bath. Under routine conditions, soaps and detergents can damage a bird's feathers by removing beneficial oils, so hold the shampoo during your

cockatiel's normal bath! If water won't do it, take him to your vet.

Let your bird bathe early in the day so his feathers can dry completely before bedtime. In cooler weather, you may want help the process along by drying your pet off with a blow-dryer to prevent him from becoming chilled after his bath. To do this, set the blow-dryer on low and keep it moving so that your bird doesn't become overheated. Your bird may soon learn (as mine has) that drying off is the most enjoyable part of his bath!

While we're discussing grooming and feather care, please don't purchase mite protectors that hang on a

*Bathtime is a favorite time for your cockatiel.*

bird's cage or conditioning products that are applied directly to a bird's feathers. Well-cared-for cockatiels don't have mites and shouldn't be in danger of contracting them. (If your pet does have mites, veterinary care is the most effective treatment method.) Also, the fumes from some of these products are quite strong and can be harmful to your pet's health. Conditioners, anti-picking products and other substances that are applied to your bird's feathers will serve one purpose: to get your bird to preen himself so thoroughly that he could remove all his feathers in a particular area. If you want to encourage your bird to preen regularly and help condition his feathers, simply mist the bird regularly with clean, warm water or hold him under a gentle stream from a kitchen or bathroom faucet. Your bird will take care of the rest.

## NAIL CARE

Cockatiels and other parrots need their nails clipped occasionally to prevent the nails from catching on toys or perches and injuring the bird.

You will need to remove only tiny portions of the nail to keep your cockatiel's claws trimmed. Generally, a good guideline to follow is to only remove the hook on each nail, and to do this in the smallest increments possible. Stop well before you reach the quick. If you do happen to cut the nail short enough to make it bleed, apply cornstarch or flour, followed by direct pressure, to stop the bleeding.

## WING TRIMMING

Cockatiels are among the fastest flying pet birds. Their sleek, slender bodies give them an advantage over larger birds, such as Amazons and African greys. Since cockatiels are so aerodynamic, owners must pay close attention to the condition of the bird's wing feathers and trim them regularly to keep the bird safe. The goal of a proper wing trim is to prevent your pet from flying away or into a window, mirror or wall while he's out of his cage.

You may want to enlist the help of your avian veterinarian, at least the first time. Wing trimming is a task that must be performed carefully to avoid injuring your pet, so take your time if you're doing it yourself. Please do not just take up the largest pair of kitchen shears you own and start snipping away, as this can cause severe injury to the bird's wing tips.

## What You'll Need

The first step in wing feather trimming is to assemble your supplies and find a quiet, well-lit place to groom your pet before you catch him. Your grooming tools will include

- a well-worn washcloth or small towel to wrap your bird in

- small, sharp scissors to do the actual trimming

- needle-nosed pliers (to pull any blood feathers you may cut accidentally)

- flour or cornstarch to act as styptic powder in case a blood feather is cut

I encourage you to groom your pet in a quiet, well-lit place because grooming excites some birds and causes them to become wiggly. Having good light to work under will make your job easier, and having

*You may want to trim your cockatiel's wings to keep him from flying away.*

a quiet work area may calm your pet and make him more handleable.

## Getting Started

Once you've assembled your supplies, drape the towel over your hand and catch your bird with your toweled hand. Hold your bird by the back of his head and neck, and wrap him in the towel to prevent him from flopping his wings. Support your bird's head securely with your thumb and index finger. (Having the bird's head covered by the towel will

*If your cockatiel is used to being handled, he shouldn't mind having his wings trimmed.*

calm him and will give him something to chew on while you clip his wings.) If your fingers get close to her beak, he will bite you. A frightened or angry bird will bite even the human he loves the best. If he bites you, gently reposition your fingers so he cannot reach them. You may need to pry his beak open—carefully. Often, gentle pressure on either side of his beak will cause him to open it. Grasp your bird in your left hand, your thumb and middle finger steading his head. With your right hand, gently extend his left wing. Check carefully for feathers that are still growing in.

These can be identified by their waxy, tight look and their dark centers or quills, which are caused by the blood supply to the new feather.

## Careful Trimming

If your bird has a number of blood feathers, you may want to put off trimming his wings for a few days, because fully grown feathers cushion those just coming in from hard knocks. If your bird has only one or two blood feathers, you can trim the rest accordingly. Secure the bird as before and anchor the wing between your fourth finger and smallest finger.

To trim your bird's feathers, separate each one away from the other flight feathers and cut it individually (remember, the goal is to have a well-trimmed bird that's still able to glide a bit if he needs to). Use the primary coverts (the set of feathers above the primary flight feathers on your bird's wing) as a safe guideline to monitor how short you can trim.

Cut the first six to eight flight feathers starting from the tip of the wing, and be sure to trim an equal number of feathers from each wing. Although some people think that a bird needs only one trimmed wing, this is incorrect and could actually cause harm to a bird that tries to fly with one trimmed and one untrimmed wing. Remember to check your bird's wing feathers and retrim them periodically (about four times a year as a minimum).

# ABOUT BLOOD FEATHERS

If you do happen to cut a blood feather, remain calm. You must remove it and stop the bleeding. Take a pair of needle-nosed pliers and grasp the broken feather's shaft as close to the skin of your bird's wing as you can. With one steady motion, pull the feather out completely. After you've removed the feather, put a pinch of flour or cornstarch on the feather follicle (the spot you pulled the feather out of) and apply direct pressure for a few minutes until the bleeding stops. If the bleeding doesn't stop after a few minutes of direct pressure, or if you can't remove the feather shaft, contact your avian veterinarian for further instructions.

Although it may seem like you're hurting your cockatiel by removing the broken blood feather, consider this: A broken blood feather is like an open faucet. If the feather stays in, the faucet remains open and lets the blood out. Once removed, the bird's skin generally closes up behind the feather shaft and shuts off the faucet.

Be particularly alert after a molt, because your bird will have a whole new crop of flight feathers that need attention. You'll be able to tell when your bird is due for a trim when he starts becoming bolder in his flying attempts. Right after a wing trim, a cockatiel generally tries to fly and finds he's unsuccessful at the attempt. He will keep trying, though, and may surprise you one day with a fairly good glide across his cage or off his play gym. If this happens, get the scissors and trim those wings immediately.

# CHAPTER SIX

# To Good Health

In general, cockatiels have a hardy resistance to disease and are very healthy birds. They have a strong survival instinct, and even when ill, cockatiels will continue to "act" normally for long periods of time. Since birds can't describe how they are feeling, it is very important that owners understand the basics of their pet's physiology as well as the signs of illness. Cockatiels, like all other pets, are subject to disease and injury. With preventive measures, early detection and good care, the odds for successful recovery are great.

## AVIAN ANATOMY

Your pet cockatiel's body is essentially very similar to that of a mammal.

Both have skin, skeletons, respiratory, cardiovascular, digestive, excretory and nervous systems and sensory organs, although the various systems function in slightly different ways.

### Skin

Your bird's skin is difficult to see since your pet has so many feathers.

If you part the feathers carefully, though, you can see thin, seemingly transparent skin and the muscles beneath it. Modified skin cells help make up your bird's beak, cere, claws and the scales on her feet and legs.

Birds cannot perspire as mammals do because birds have no sweat glands, so they must have a way to cool themselves off. On a warm day, you may notice your bird sitting with her wings held away from her body, rolling her tongue and holding her mouth open. This is how a bird cools herself off. Watch your bird

*Feathers are amazing things, helping birds fly, keep warm and attract mates.*

carefully on warm days because she can overheat quickly, and may suffer from heatstroke, which requires veterinary care. If you live in a warm climate, ask your avian veterinarian how you can protect your bird from this serious problem.

Feathers help birds fly, they keep birds warm, they attract the attention of potential mates and they help scare away predators.

Did you know that your cockatiel has between 5,000 and 6,000 feathers on her body? These feathers grow from follicles that are arranged in rows that are known as pterylae. The unfeathered patches of bare skin on your bird's body are called apteria.

A feather is a remarkable thing. The base of the feather shaft, which fits into the bird's skin, is called the quill. It is light and hollow, but remarkably tough. The upper part of the feather shaft is called the rachis. From the rachis branch the barbs and barbules (smaller barbs) that make up most of the feather. The barbs and barbules have small hooks on them that enable the different parts of the feather to interlock like Velcro and form the feather's vane or web.

Birds have several different types of feathers on their bodies. *Contour feathers* are the colorful outer feathers on a bird's body and wings. Many birds have an undercoating of *down feathers* that helps keep them warm. *Semiplume feathers* are found on a bird's beak, nares (nostrils) and eyelids.

A bird's *flight feathers* can be classified into one of two types. Primary flight feathers are the large wing feathers that push a bird forward during flight. They are also the ones that need clipping, which we discussed earlier. Secondary flight feathers are found on the inner wing, and they help support the bird in flight. Primary and secondary wing feathers can operate independently of each other. The bird's tail feathers also assist in flight by acting as a brake and a rudder to make steering easier.

To keep their feathers in good condition, healthy birds spend a great deal of time fluffing and preening. You may see your cockatiel seeming to pick at the base of her tail on the top side. This is a normal behavior in which the bird removes oil from the preen gland and spreads it on her feathers. The oil helps

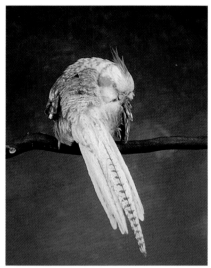

*Preening keeps feathers healthy.*

prevent skin infections and waterproofs the feathers.

Sometimes pet birds will develop white lines or small holes on the large feathers of their wings and tails. These lines or holes are referred to as "stress bars" or "stress lines" and result from the bird being under stress as the feathers were developing. If you notice stress bars on your bird's feathers, discuss them with your avian veterinarian.

## Musculoskeletal System

Did you know that some bird bones are hollow? These are lighter, which makes flying easier, but they are also more susceptible to breakage. For this reason, you must always handle your bird carefully! Another adaptation for flight is that the bones of a bird's wing (which correspond to our arm and hand bones) are fused for greater strength.

Birds also have air sacs in some of their bones (these are called pneumatic bones) and in certain body cavities that help lighten the bird's body and also cool her more efficiently.

Parrots have ten neck vertebrae to a human's seven. This makes a parrot's neck more mobile than a person's (a parrot can turn its head almost 180°), and gives the parrot an advantage in spotting food or predators in the wild.

## Respiratory System

Your bird's respiratory system is a highly efficient system that works in a markedly different way from yours. Here's how your bird breathes: Air enters the system through your bird's nares, passes through her sinuses and into her throat. As it does, the air is filtered through the choana, which is a slit that can be easily seen in the roof of many birds' mouths. The choana also helps to clean and warm the air.

After the air passes the choana, it flows through the larynx and trachea, past the syrinx or "voice box." Your bird doesn't have vocal cords like you do; rather, vibrations of the syrinx membrane are what allow birds to make sounds. As the air continues its journey past the syrinx and into the bronchi, your bird's lungs don't expand and contract to bring the air in. This is partly due to the fact that birds don't have diaphragms like people do. Instead,

*Air enters your cockatiel's body through her nares, or nostrils.*

the bird's body wall expands and contracts, much like a fireplace bellows. This action brings air into the air sacs mentioned earlier as part of the skeleton. This bellows action also moves air in and out of the lungs—two complete breaths are required to do the same work as a single breath in people and other mammals. This is why you may notice that your bird seems to be breathing quite quickly.

## Digestive System

A parrot's mouth works differently than a mammal's. Parrots don't have saliva to break down and move their food like we do. After the food leaves your bird's mouth, it travels down the esophagus, where it is moistened. The food then travels to the crop, where it is moistened further and emptied in small increments into the bird's stomach.

After the food leaves the crop, it travels through the proventriculus, where digestive juices are added, then to the gizzard, where the food is broken down into even smaller pieces. The food next travels to the small intestine, where nutrients are absorbed into the bloodstream.

Anything that's left over travels through the large intestine to the cloaca, which is the common chamber that collects wastes before they leave the bird's body through the vent. The whole process from mouth to vent usually takes only a few hours, which is why you may notice that your bird leaves frequent, small droppings in her cage.

Along with the solid waste created by the digestive system, your cockatiel's kidneys create urine, which is transported through ureters to the cloaca for excretion. Unlike a mammal, a bird does not have a bladder or a urethra.

## Nervous System

### YOUR BIRD'S SENSES

TASTE—Compared to other mammals, the sense of taste is poorly developed in cockatiels due to the small number and location of taste buds (on the roof of the mouth rather than the tongue).

VISION—Cockatiels have a well-developed sense of sight. Birds see detail and they can discern colors. Because their eyes are located on the sides of their heads, most pet birds

*Because they don't have many taste buds, cockatiels' sense of taste is not highly developed.*

rely on monocular vision, which means that they use each eye independent of the other. If a bird wants to study an object, you will see her tilt her head to one side and examine the object with just one eye. Birds aren't really able to move their eyes around very much, but they compensate for this by having highly mobile necks.

Like cats and dogs, birds have third eyelids called nictitating membranes that you will sometimes see flick briefly across your cockatiel's eye. The purpose of this membrane is to keep the eyeball moist and clean. If you see your cockatiel's

nictitating membrane for more than a brief second, contact your avian veterinarian for an evaluation. You have probably noticed that your bird lacks eyelashes. In their place are small feathers called semiplumes that help keep dirt and dust out of the bird's eyeball.

**HEARING**—You may be wondering where your bird's ears are. Look carefully under the feathers behind and below each eye to find them. The ears are somewhat large holes in the sides of your bird's head. Cockatiels have about the same ability to distinguish sound waves and determine the location of the sound as people do, but birds seem to be less sensitive to higher and lower pitches than their owners.

SMELL—You may be wondering how your pet's sense of smell compares to your own. Birds seem to have poorly developed senses of smell because smells often dissipate quickly in the air (where flying birds spend the majority of their time).

TOUCH—The final sense we relate to, touch, is well-developed in parrots. Parrots use their feet and their mouths to touch their surroundings (young birds particularly seem to "mouth" everything they can get their beaks on), to play and to determine what is safe to perch on or chew on and what's good to eat.

Along with their tactile uses, a parrot's feet also have an unusual design compared to other caged birds. Unlike a finch, the cockatiel's toes point forward and two point backward in an arrangement called zygodactyl. This allows a parrot to climb up, down and around trees easily. Some larger parrots also use their feet to hold food or to play with toys.

*Cockatiels enjoy being gently stroked by their friends.*

# HEALTH CARE

With good care, a cockatiel can live about twenty years or more.

## *Visiting the Veterinarian*

As a caring owner, you want your bird to have the best chance at living a long, healthy life. To that end, you will need to locate a veterinarian who understands the special medical needs of birds and with whom you can establish a good working relationship. The best time to do this is when you first bring your cockatiel home from the breeder or pet store. If possible, arrange to visit your veterinarian's office on your way home from the breeder or store. This is particularly important if you have other birds at home, because you don't want to endanger the health of your existing flock or your new pet.

### THE PHYSICAL EXAM

After the question-and-answer session with you, the exam will begin. Your veterinarian will probably take his first look at your cockatiel while she is still in her cage or carrier. The veterinarian does this to give the

*Soon after you get your cock-atiel, schedule a visit to your avian veterinar-ian to have her examined.*

bird an opportunity to become accustomed to him, rather than simply reaching right in and grabbing your pet. While the veterinarian is talking to you, he will check the bird's feather condition, her overall appearance, posture and perching ability.

Next, the doctor will drape a towel over his hand and gently catch your cockatiel and remove her from her carrier or cage. When the bird is out of her carrier, the doctor will look her over carefully. He will note the condition of your pet's eyes, her beak and her nares (nostrils). He will weigh your bird in a device that looks like a metal colander balanced on a scale, and the doctor will feel, or palpate, your bird's body, wings, legs and feet for any abnormalities.

## Common Avian Tests

After your veterinarian has completed the physical examination, further tests may be recommended:

- Blood workups, which can be further broken down into a complete blood count that determines how many platelets, red and white blood cells your bird has (this

## COMMON VETERINARY QUERIES

In addition to reviewing a patient form, the veterinarian will ask you a few questions that will help him get to know your bird. These may include:

- Why is the bird here today?
- What's the bird's normal activity level like?
- How is the bird's appetite?
- What does the bird's normal diet consist of?
- Have you noticed a change in the bird's appearance lately?

Be sure to explain any changes in as much detail as you can, because changes in your bird's normal behavior can indicate illness. Be aware of your bird's normal activities. Changes can signal illness, and you'll want to take action right away.

67

information can help diagnose infections or anemia), and a blood chemistry profile, which helps a veterinarian analyze how your bird's body processes enzymes, electrolytes and other chemicals.

- X-rays, which allow a veterinarian to study a bird's internal organs and bones. X-rays also help

## WHAT TO AVOID

In *The Complete Bird Owner's Handbook,* veterinarian Gary Gallerstein offers the following "don'ts" to bird owners whose birds need urgent care:

- Don't give a bird human medications or medications prescribed for another animal unless so directed by your veterinarian.

- Don't give your bird medications that are suggested by a friend, a store employee or a human physician.

- Don't give a bird alcohol or laxatives.

- Don't apply any oils or ointments to your bird unless your veterinarian tells you to do so.

- Don't bathe a sick bird. Your calm demeanor will soothe and decrease the stress of an ill or injured cockatiel. Taking good care of your cockatiel will help bond you with your bird.

doctors find foreign bodies in a bird's system.

- Microbiological exams, which help determine if any unusual organisms (bacteria, fungi or yeast) are growing inside your bird's body.

- Fecal analysis, which studies a small sample of your bird's

droppings to determine if she has internal parasites, or a bacterial or yeast infection.

## MEDICATING YOUR COCKATIEL

Most bird owners will have to medicate their pets at some point in the birds' lives, and many are unsure if they can complete the task without hurting their birds. If you have to medicate your pet, your avian veterinarian or veterinary technician should explain the process to you.

Let's briefly review the most common method of administering medications to birds, which is discussed completely in *The Complete Bird Owner's Handbook* by Gary A. Gallerstein, DVM.

**BY MOUTH:** This is a good route to take with birds that are small, easy to handle or underweight. The medication is usually given with a needleless plastic syringe placed in the left side of the bird's mouth and pointed toward the right side of her throat. This route is recommended to ensure that the medication gets into the bird's digestive system and not into her lungs, where aspiration pneumonia can result.

## Cockatiel Health Concerns

Although cockatiels are generally hardy birds, they are prone to a few health problems, including giardia, conjunctivitis, candida, roundworms and papillomas. They, like all birds, can also suffer from respiratory problems and other conditions that result from a vitamin A deficiency, especially if they consume diets that are high in seeds and low in vitamin-A–rich foods. Vitamin A deficiency can be prevented by feeding a varied, healthy diet.

## Giardiasis

Giardiasis is caused by a protozoan called Giardia psittaci. Signs of a giardia infection include loose droppings, weight loss, feather picking (especially under the wings), loss of appetite and depression. Your avian veterinarian may have difficulty diagnosing this disease because the giardia organism is difficult to detect in a bird's feces. The disease can be spread through contaminated food or water, and birds are not immune to it once they've had it. Your veterinarian can recommend an appropriate medication to treat giardia.

## Conjunctivitis

Cockatiel conjunctivitis is seen in white or albino birds more than in normal grays. Signs include inflammation of the eyelid and discharge from the eye with no apparent cause. Treatment with topical antibiotic ointment resolves the signs temporarily, but recurrences are

*Cockatiels—especially white ones—can develop an inflammation of the eye called conjunctivitis. This bird is healthy.*

common. Affected birds should not be used in breeding programs because there is some evidence that this is a genetic problem.

## Candida

Cockatiel breeders need to pay particular attention to candida, which is caused by the yeast Candida albicans. Young cockatiels seem to be particularly susceptible to candida infestations, which occur when a bird's diet is low in vitamin A. Signs of candida include white, cheesy growths in the bird's mouth and throat; a loss of appetite;

regurgitation or vomiting; and a crop that is slow to empty.

The trouble with trying to diagnose a candida infestation is that many adult cockatiels don't show any signs of the condition, so a breeder may not even know he or she has infected birds until the parent birds pass the yeast to the chicks during feeding. Hand-fed chicks are not immune to the condition, either, because they can be affected by it if their throats are damaged by feeding tubes. Veterinary assistance in the form of antifungal drugs and a diet high in vitamin A may be your best weapons against candida.

*Feather plucking can lead to unsightly and unhealthy baldness.*

## Roundworms

Roundworms, or ascarids, can infest cockatiels that have access to dirt, which is where roundworm eggs are found. The worms themselves are 2 to 5 inches long and resemble white spaghetti. Mild infestations of roundworms can cause weight loss, appetite loss, growth abnormalities and diarrhea, while heavy infestations can result in bowel blockage and death.

To diagnose roundworms, your veterinarian will analyze a sample of your bird's droppings. He or she can then prescribe an appropriate course of treatment to clear up the problem.

## *Papillomas*

Papillomas are benign tumors that can appear almost anywhere on a bird's skin, including her foot, leg, eyelid or preen gland. If a bird has a papilloma on her cloaca, the bird may appear to have a "wet raspberry" coming out of her vent. These tumors, which are caused by a virus, can appear as small, crusty lesions, or they may be raised growths that have a bumpy texture or small projections.

Many papillomas can be left untreated without harm to the bird, but some must be removed by an avian veterinarian because a bird may pick at the growth and cause it to bleed.

## *Bald Spots*

Although it isn't a health problem per se, some cockatiels, particularly lutinos, are prone to bald spots behind their crests. These spots resulted from inbreeding cockatiels to create the mutation in the 1950s. Birds with noticeable bald spots on

## SIGNS OF ILLNESS

If your bird shows any of these signs, contact your veterinarian immediately for further instructions. Your bird should be seen as soon as possible.

- a fluffed-up appearance
- a loss of appetite
- the bird wants to sleep all the time
- a change in the appearance or number of droppings
- weight loss
- listlessness
- drooping wings
- lameness
- the bird has partially eaten food stuck to her face or food has been regurgitated onto the cage floor
- labored breathing, with or without tail bobbing
- runny eyes or nose
- the bird stops whistling
- productive sneezing

71

the backs of their heads are generally held out of breeding programs to try to ensure that the trait doesn't get passed on to future generations.

Psittacine beak and feather disease syndrome (PBFDS) has been a hot topic among bird keepers for the last decade. The virus was first detected in cockatoos and was originally thought to be a cockatoo-specific problem. It has since been determined that more than forty species of parrots, including cockatiels, can contract this disease, which causes a bird's feathers to become pinched or clubbed in appearance. Other symptoms include beak fractures and mouth ulcers. This highly contagious, fatal disease is most common in birds less than 3 years of age, and there is no cure at present. A vaccine is under development at the University of Georgia.

## COCKATIEL FIRST AID

Sometimes your pet will get herself into a situation that will require quick thinking and even quicker action on your part to help save your bird from serious injury or death. Learning basic first aid techniques may prove to be useful in these situations.

## Basic Supplies

Assemble a bird owner's first-aid kit so that you will have some basic supplies on hand before your bird needs them. Here's what to include:

- appropriate-sized towels for catching and holding your bird
- a heating pad, heat lamp or other heat source
- a pad of paper and pencil to make notes about bird's condition
- styptic powder, silver nitrate stick or cornstarch to stop bleeding (use styptic powder and silver nitrate stick on beak and nails only)
- blunt-tipped scissors
- nail clippers and nail file
- needle-nosed pliers to pull broken blood feathers
- blunt-end tweezers
- hydrogen peroxide or other disinfectant solution
- eye irrigation solution
- bandage materials such as gauze squares, masking tape (it doesn't stick to a bird's feathers like adhesive tape does) and gauze rolls
- Pedialyte or other energy supplement

- eye dropper
- syringes to irrigate wounds or feed sick birds
- penlight

Keep all these supplies in one place, such as a fishing tackle box. This will eliminate having to search for supplies in emergency situations, and the case can be taken along to bird shows, on trips or left for the bird sitter.

You should familiarize your cockatiel with a travel case should you need to transport her in an emergency. It should be one made for birds with a perch low to the cage bottom. If you use a general carrier made for dogs or cats, do not attempt to put a perch in the case. Instead, cover the bottom with clean black and white newspapers. Offer your bird fruit and water.

*Emergency or not, your cockatiel will be calmer if you're calm.*

## First, Stabilize

No matter what the situation, there are a few things to keep in mind when facing a medical emergency with your pet. First, keep as calm as possible to lessen the shock of injury and to reassure your pet. Next, stop any bleeding, keep the bird warm and minimize handling her.

After you've stabilized your pet, call your veterinarian's office for further instructions. Tell them "This is an emergency" and that your bird has had an accident. Describe what happened to your pet as clearly and calmly as you can. Listen carefully to the instructions you are given and

*You should familiarize your cockatiel with a travel case should you need to transport her in an emergency.*

follow them. Finally, transport your bird to the vet's office as quickly and safely as you can.

# MEDICAL EMERGENCIES

Here are some urgent medical situations that bird owners are likely to encounter, the reason that they are medical emergencies, the signs and symptoms your bird might show, and the recommended treatments for the problem:

## Beak Injury

*It's an emergency because:* A bird needs both her upper and lower beak (also called the upper and lower mandible) to eat and preen properly. Infections can also set in rather quickly if a beak is fractured or punctured.

*Signs:* Bird is bleeding from her beak. This often occurs after the bird flies into a windowpane or mirror, or if she has a run-in with an operational ceiling fan. Bird may have also cracked or damaged her beak, and portions of the beak may be missing.

*Steps to take:* Control bleeding. Keep bird calm and quiet. Contact your avian veterinarian's office.

## Bleeding

*It's an emergency because:* A bird can withstand only about a 20 percent loss of blood volume and still recover from an injury.

*Signs:* In the event of external bleeding, you will see blood on the bird, her cage and her surroundings. In the case of internal bleeding, the bird may pass bloody droppings or bleed from her nose, mouth or vent.

*Steps to take:* For external bleeding, apply direct pressure. If the bleeding doesn't stop with direct pressure, apply a coagulant, such as styptic powder (for nails and beaks) or cornstarch (for broken feathers and skin injuries).

If the bleeding stops, observe the bird for restarting of the bleeding or for shock. Call your veterinarian's office if the bird seems weak or if she has lost a lot of blood and arrange to take the bird in for further treatment.

## Breathing Problems

*It's an emergency because:* Respiratory problems in pet birds can be life threatening.

*Signs:* The bird wheezes or clicks while breathing, bobs her tail,

*This inquisitive youngster doesn't have any breathing problems.*

breathes with an open mouth, has discharge from her nares or swelling around her eyes.

*Steps to take:* Keep the bird warm, place her in a bathroom with a hot shower running to help her breathe easier and call your veterinarian's office.

## Cloacal Prolapse

*It's an emergency because:* The bird's lower intestines, uterus or cloaca is protruding from the bird's vent.

*Signs:* The bird has pink, red, brown or black tissue protruding from her vent.

*If you have a breeding pair, keep a close eye on the female, who may suffer egg binding.*

*Steps to take:* Contact your veterinarian's office for immediate follow-up care. Your veterinarian can usually reposition the organs.

## Egg Binding

*It's an emergency because:* The egg blocks the hen's excretory system and makes it impossible for her to eliminate.

Eggs can sometimes break inside the hen, which can lead to infection.

*Signs:* An egg-bound hen strains to lay eggs unsuccessfully. She becomes fluffed and lethargic, sits on the floor of her cage, may be paralyzed and may have a swollen abdomen.

*Steps to take:* Keep the hen warm as this sometimes helps her pass the egg. Put her and her cage into a warm bathroom with a hot shower running to increase the humidity, which may help her pass the egg. If your bird doesn't improve shortly (within a hour), contact your vet.

## Eye Injury

*It's an emergency because:* Untreated eye problems may lead to blindness.

*Signs:* Swollen or pasty eyelids, discharge, cloudy eyeball, increased rubbing of eye area.

*Steps to take:* Examine the eye carefully for foreign bodies. Contact your veterinarian for more information.

## Inhaled or Eaten Foreign Object

*It's an emergency because:* Birds can develop serious respiratory or digestive problems from foreign objects in their bodies.

*Signs:* In the case of inhaled items, wheezing and other respiratory problems. In the case of consumed objects, the bird was seen playing with a small item that suddenly cannot be found.

*Steps to take:* If you suspect that your bird has inhaled or eaten something she shouldn't, contact your veterinarian's office immediately.

## Overheating

*It's an emergency because:* High body temperatures can kill a bird.

*Signs:* An overheated bird will try to make herself thin. She will hold her wings away from her body, open her mouth and roll her tongue in an attempt to cool herself. Birds don't have sweat glands, so they must try to cool their bodies by exposing as much of their skin's surface as they can to moving air.

*Steps to take:* Cool the bird off by putting her in front of a fan (make sure the blades are screened so the bird doesn't injure herself further), by spraying her with cool water or by having her stand in a bowl of cool water. Let the bird drink cool water if she can (if she can't, offer her cool water with an eyedropper) and contact your veterinarian.

## Poisoning

*It's an emergency because:* Poisons can kill a bird quickly.

*Signs:* Poisoned birds may suddenly regurgitate, have diarrhea or bloody droppings and have redness or burns around their mouths. They may also go into convulsions, become paralyzed or go into shock.

*Steps to take:* Put the poison out of your bird's reach. Contact your veterinarian for further instructions. Be prepared to take the poison with you to the vet's office in case he or she needs to contact a poison control center for further information.

## Seizures

*It's an emergency because:* Seizures can indicate a number of serious

*A number of household items can send your bird into shock if you don't safeguard him.*

conditions, including lead poisoning, infections, nutritional deficiency, heat stroke and epilepsy.

*Signs:* The bird goes into a seizure that lasts from a few seconds to a minute. Afterward, she seems dazed and may stay on the cage floor for several hours. She also appear unsteady and won't perch.

*Steps to take:* Keep the bird from hurting herself further by removing everything you can from her cage. Cover the bird's cage with a towel and darken the room to reduce the bird's stress level. Contact your veterinarian's office for further instructions immediately.

## Shock

*It's an emergency because:* Shock indicates that the bird's circulatory system cannot move the blood supply around the bird's body. This is a serious condition that can lead to death if left untreated.

*Signs:* Shocky birds may act depressed, breathe rapidly and have a fluffed appearance. If your bird displays these signs in conjunction with a recent accident, suspect shock and take appropriate action.

*Steps to take:* Keep your bird warm, cover her cage and transport her to your veterinarian's office as soon as possible.

Veterinarian Michael Murray recommends that bird owners keep the following tips in mind when facing emergency situations:

Keep the bird warm. You can do this by putting the bird in an empty aquarium with a heating pad under her, by putting a heat lamp near the bird's cage or by putting a heating pad set on low under the bird's cage in place of the cage tray. Whatever heat source you choose to use, make sure to keep a close eye on your bird so that she doesn't accidentally burn herself on the pad or lamp and that she doesn't chew on a power cord.

Put the bird in a dark, quiet room. This helps reduce the bird's stress.

Put the bird's food in locations that are easy to reach. Sick birds need to eat, but they may not be able to reach food in its normal locations in the cage. Sometimes, birds require hand-feeding to keep their calorie consumption steady.

Protect the bird from additional injury. If the convalescing bird is in a clear-sided aquarium, for example, you may want to put a towel over the glass to keep the bird from flying into it.

# PREVENTIVE CARE

Your cockatiel requires a certain level of care each day to ensure her health and well-being. Here are some of the things you'll need to do each day for your pet:

- Observe your pet for any changes in her routine (report any changes to your avian veterinarian immediately).

- Offer fresh food and remove old food. Wash and rinse food dish thoroughly. Rinse thoroughly and allow to dry.

- Check seed dish and refill as necessary with clean, fresh seed.

- Provide fresh water and remove previous dish. Wash dish as above.

- Change paper in cage tray.

- Let the bird out of her cage for supervised playtime.

- Finally, you'll want to cover your bird's cage at about the same time every night to indicate bedtime.

Cockatiels, like all parrots, seem to enjoy a familiar routine. When you cover the cage, you'll probably hear your bird rustling around for a bit, perhaps getting a drink of water or a last mouthful of seeds before settling in for the night. Keep in mind that your pet will require eight to ten hours of sleep a day, but you can expect that she will take naps during the day to supplement her nightly snooze.

## Monitor Droppings

Although it may seem a bit unpleasant to discuss, your bird's droppings require daily monitoring because they can tell you a lot about her general health.

Cockatiels produce white-and-green tubular droppings. These droppings are usually composed of equal amounts of fecal material (the green portion), urine (a clear liquid portion) and urates (the white or cream-colored part).

*Part of regular preventive care is careful observation of your bird.*

A healthy cockatiel generally eliminates about every fifteen minutes, although your bird may go more or less often.

Texture and consistency, along with frequency or lack of droppings, can let you know how your pet is feeling. For instance, if a bird eats a lot of fruits and vegetables, her droppings are generally looser and more watery than a bird that eats primarily seeds. But watery droppings can also indicate illness, such as diabetes or kidney problems, that cause a bird to drink more water than usual.

Color can also give an indication of health. Birds that have psittacosis typically have bright, lime-green droppings, while healthy birds have avocado or darker green and white droppings. Birds with liver problems may produce droppings that are yellowish or reddish, while birds that have internal bleeding will produce dark, tarry droppings.

A color change doesn't necessarily indicate poor health in your cockatiel. For instance, birds that eat pelleted diets tend to have darker droppings than their seed-eating companions, while parrots that have splurged on a certain fresh food soon have droppings with that characteristic color.

## Weekly Chores

The following chores should be done on a weekly basis to keep your cockatiel healthy and happy:

- Removing old food from cage bars and from the corners of the cage where it invariably falls.

- Removing, scraping and replacing the perches to keep them clean and free of debris (you might also want to sand them lightly with coarse grain sandpaper to clean them further and improve perch traction for your bird).

- Rotating toys in your bird's cage to keep them interesting. Remember to discard any toys that show excessive signs of wear (frayed rope, cracked plastic or well-chewed wood).

## CAGE CLEANING TIPS

You can simplify the weekly cage cleaning process by placing the cage in the shower and letting hot water from the showerhead do some of the work. Be sure to remove your bird, her food and water dishes, the cage tray paper and her toys before putting the cage into the shower. You can let the hot water run over the cage for a few minutes, then scrub at any stuck-on food with an old toothbrush or some fine-grade

81

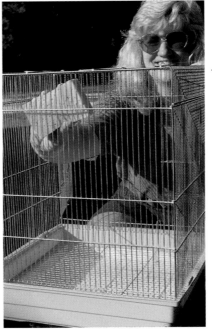

*Give your bird's cage a thorough scrubbing every few weeks.*

## COMFORT DURING MOLTING

- encourage balanced nutrition
- decrease stress by emphasizing security and rest periods
- keep room temperature between 75° and 80°F during heavy molting
- promote preening activity

steel wool. After you've removed the food and other debris, you can disinfect the cage with a spray-on disinfectant that you can purchase at your pet store. Make sure to choose a bird-safe product, and read the instructions completely before use.

Rinse the cage thoroughly and dry it completely before returning your bird and her accessories to the cage. (If you have wooden perches in the cage, you can dry them more quickly by placing the wet dowels in a 400°F oven for ten minutes. Let the perches cool before you put them back in the cage.)

## REGULATE TEMPERATURE

Warm weather requires a little extra vigilance on the part of a pet bird owner to ensure that your pet remains comfortable even in hot weather. To help keep your pet cool, keep her out of direct sun, offer her lots of fresh, juicy vegetables and fruits (be sure to remove these fresh foods from the cage promptly to prevent your bird from eating spoiled food) and mist her lightly with a clean spray bottle (filled with water only) that is used solely for showering your bird.

By the same token, pay attention to your pet's needs when the weather turns cooler. You may want to use a heavier cage cover, especially if you lower the heat in your home at bedtime, or you may want to move the bird's cage to another location in your home that is warmer and less drafty.

## ABOUT MOLTING

At least once a year, your cockatiel will lose her feathers. Don't be alarmed, because this is a normal process called molting. Many pet birds seem to be in a perpetual molt, with feathers falling out and coming in throughout the summer.

You can consider your bird in molting season when you see a lot of whole feathers in the bottom of the cage and you notice that your bird seems to have broken out in a rash of stubby little aglets (the plastic tips on the ends of your shoelaces). These pinfeather sheaths help new feathers break through the skin, and they are made of keratin. The sheaths also help protect growing feathers from damage until the feather completes its growth cycle.

You may notice that your cockatiel is a little more irritable during the molt; this is to be expected. Think about how you would feel if you had all these itchy new feathers coming. However, your bird may actively seek out more time with you during the molt because owners are handy to have around when a cockatiel has an itch on the top of her head that she can't quite scratch! (Scratch these new feathers gently because some of them may

*Your cockatiel will "molt" her feathers about once a year.*

still be growing in and may be sensitive to the touch.) Some birds may benefit from special conditioning foods during the molt; check with your avian veterinarian to see if your bird is a candidate for these foods.

# CHAPTER SEVEN

# A Matter of Fact

Second in popularity only to budgies, cockatiels have charmed many people. Some say it's their small size or affordable price that makes cockatiels so appealing, while others cite their appearance or personalities. Others are captivated by the cockatiel's whistling abilities, cleanliness and long potential life span. Finally, many bird owners are attracted to the cockatiel's curiosity and adaptability.

In any case, cockatiels can be wonderful pets that reward their owners with years of entertainment and companionship. In return for this love, a cockatiel requires care and attention from his owner.

## THE COCKATIEL'S BACKGROUND

"Although one of the most soberly coloured members of the parrot family, the cockatiel has long been popular among aviculturists by reason of its hardiness, prolificacy and gentle disposition," wrote the noted aviculturist, the Duke of Bedford, in his book, *Parrots and Parrot-like Birds,* in the early 1950s. The cockatiel is still popular some forty years later. According to statistics from the American Pet Product Manufacturer Association, about 16 million pet birds are kept in American homes, and 34 percent of them are cockatiels.

The cockatiel originated in Australia, which is home to some parrot species. In his homeland, the cockatiel is sometimes called the quarrion, the weero, the cockatoo parrot or the crested parrot. Small flocks of two to twelve feed on seedling grasses and other plants. Their habitats can range from open eucalyptus savannas to arid grasslands. Cockatiel flocks depend on rainfall for water and, once a steady supply of food and water are avail-

*The cockatiel's small size, affordable price and numerous abilities and talents have made this bird second in popularity only to budgies.*

able, to establish the start of the breeding season.

In the wild, cockatiels are active during the early morning and the late afternoon. These are the times they usually head toward a water source to drink, being sure to leave quickly rather than become a meal for a passing bird of prey. They spend a good bit of their day on the ground, searching for food, but they are likely to spend midday blending into their surroundings by sitting lengthwise along dead tree branches that are free of foliage.

The cockatiel was first described by naturalists who visited Australia with Captain James Cook in 1770, and the first specimen may have come to the Royal College of Surgeons Museum in England as a result of this trip. The Australian government imposed a ban on exporting all native birds in 1894, so the cockatiels kept in North America and Europe have resulted from domestic breeding efforts in those countries for more than 100 years.

## COCKATIEL OR COCKATOO?

Many consider the cockatiel to be the smallest of the cockatoos. Here are some comparisons between

*The cockatiel originated in Australia and is revered for his gentle disposition.*

cockatiels (true parrots) and cockatoos. Do you agree?

## Characteristics Cockatiels Share with Cockatoos

- Crests.
- Cockatiel hens and some cockatoos have bars on the undersides of their tail feathers.
- Male and female birds alternate incubation duties.
- Both parents feed chicks.
- Cheek patches occur in cockatiels and some cockatoos.
- Cockatiels and cockatoos both make dramatic, sweeping beak movements, followed by holding the head back, when drinking.
- Cockatiels and cockatoos make similar noises while eating.
- First down feathers of the young are yellow.
- First plumage changes completely after first molt.
- Both cockatiel and cockatoo chicks remain partially naked before their feathers come in.
- Cockatiels and most cockatoos don't engage in courtship displays,

*Many cockatiels have color combinations of gray, white and yellow.*

such as the male feeding the female.

- Cockatiels and cockatoos show fear in similar ways. Birds rock slowly from side to side, hiss, fan their tails and lift the front part of the wings while keeping the wing tips close to the body.

# HOW THE COCKATIEL GOT ITS NAME

Because the cockatiel has some anatomical differences from the other seventeen members of the cockatoo family, the cockatiel has been classified into its own genus, *Nymphicus,* and has its own species name, *hollandicus.* The scientific name, which went through several variations before a naturalist named Wagler settled on its present form in 1832, translates literally to "goddess of New Holland," which is the name Australia was known by in the 1700s and 1800s.

The cockatiel's common English and American name comes from either *Dutch kakatielje,* which means "little cockatoo," or the Portuguese *cocatilho,* which means "small parrot." The first birds were exported to Europe in the late 1830s. Color mutations began to develop in the 1950s.

# CHAPTER EIGHT

# Resources

## BOOKS

For more information on bird care, look for these at your local library, bookstore or pet store:

Alderton, David. *You and Your Pet Bird.* New York: Alfred A. Knopf, 1994.

———. *A Birdkeeper's Guide to Cockatiels.* Tetra Press, 1989.

Doane, Bonnie. *My Parrot My Friend: An Owner's Guide to Parrot Behavior.* New York: Howell Book House, 1994.

———. *The Pleasure of Their Company.* New York: Howell Book House, 1998.

Gallerstein, Gary A., DVM. *The Complete Bird Owner's Handbook.* New York: Howell Book House, 1994.

Lowell, Michele. *Your Pet Bird.* New York: Henry Holt and Company, 1994.

## MAGAZINES

*Bird Talk.* Monthly magazine devoted to pet bird ownership. Subscription information: P.O. Box 57347, Boulder, CO 80322-7347.

*Bird Time.* Editorial and advertising offices: 7-L Dundas Circle, Greensboro, NC 27407.

*Bird Breeder.* Bimonthly magazine dedicated to the concerns of bird breeders who raise and sell pet birds. Subscription information: P.O. Box 420235, Palm Coast, FL 32142-0235.

*Birds USA.* Annual magazine aimed at first-time bird owners. Look for it in your local bookstore or pet store.

## ONLINE RESOURCES

Bird-specific sites have been cropping up regularly on the Internet. These sites offer pet bird owners the opportunity to share stories about their pets, along with trading helpful hints about bird care.

If you belong to an online service, look for the pet site (it's sometimes included in more general topics, such as "Hobbies and Interests," or more specifically "Pets"). If you have Internet access, ask your Web browser software to search for "cockatiels," "parrots" or "pet birds."

AMERICAN ANIMAL HOSPITAL
ASSOCIATION
http://www.healthypet.com

ASSOCIATION OF AVIAN
VETERINARIANS
AAVCTRLOFC@aol.com

AMERICAN VETERINARY MEDICAL
ASSOCIATION
http://www.avma.org/care4pets/

NATIONAL COCKATIEL SOCIETY
http://www.upatsix.com/ncs/

ONLINE PET COCKATIEL
QUESTIONS
http://www.cockatiels.org/ncs/
features/petcare.html

# VETERINARY INFORMATION

ASSOCIATION OF AVIAN
VETERINARIANS
P.O. Box 811720
Boca Raton, FL 33481

Write to this organization for a recommendation of an avian veterinarian in your area.

AMERICAN COCKATIEL SOCIETY
9527 60th Lane North
Pinellas Park, FL 34666

NATIONAL COCKATIEL SOCIETY
286 Broad St., Suite 140
Manchester, CT 06040

Publishes monthly magazine.